It's About More Than the Money

It's About More Than the Money

Investment Wisdom
for Building a Better Life

Saly A. Glassman

Vice President, Publisher: Tim Moore
Associate Publisher and Director of Marketing: Amy Neidlinger
Executive Editor: Jim Boyd
Editorial Assistant: Pamela Boland
Operations Manager: Gina Kanouse
Senior Marketing Manager: Julie Phifer
Publicity Manager: Laura Czaja
Assistant Marketing Manager: Megan Colvin
Cover Designer: Anne Jones
Managing Editor: Kristy Hart
Project Editor: Jovana San Nicolas-Shirley
Copy Editor: Apostrophe Editing Services
Proofreader: Language Logistics, LLC
Indexer: Lisa Stumpf
Compositor: Nonie Ratcliff
Manufacturing Buyer: Dan Uhrig

© 2010 by Pearson Education, Inc.
Publishing as FT Press
Upper Saddle River, New Jersey 07458

This book is sold with the understanding that neither the author nor the publisher is engaged in rendering legal, accounting, or other professional services or advice by publishing this book. Each individual situation is unique. Thus, if legal or financial advice or other expert assistance is required in a specific situation, the services of a competent professional should be sought to ensure that the situation has been evaluated carefully and appropriately. The author and the publisher disclaim any liability, loss, or risk resulting directly or indirectly, from the use or application of any of the contents of this book.

FT Press offers excellent discounts on this book when ordered in quantity for bulk purchases or special sales. For more information, please contact U.S. Corporate and Government Sales, 1-800-382-3419, corpsales@pearsontechgroup.com. For sales outside the U.S., please contact International Sales at international@pearson.com.

Company and product names mentioned herein are the trademarks or registered trademarks of their respective owners.

Printed in the United States of America

First Printing May 2010

ISBN-10: 0-13-705032-1
ISBN-13: 978-0-13-705032-1

Pearson Education LTD.
Pearson Education Australia PTY, Limited.
Pearson Education Singapore, Pte. Ltd.
Pearson Education North Asia, Ltd.
Pearson Education Canada, Ltd.
Pearson Educatión de Mexico, S.A. de C.V.
Pearson Education—Japan
Pearson Education Malaysia, Pte. Ltd.

Library of Congress Cataloging-in-Publication Data

Glassman, Saly A., 1958–
    It's about more than the money : investment wisdom for building a better life /
Saly A. Glassman.
        p. cm.
    ISBN 978-0-13-705032-1 (pbk. : alk. paper) 1. Finance, Personal. 2. Investments.
3. Money—Psychological aspects. I. Title.
    HG179.G544 2010
    332.6—dc22
                            2009051274

To my children,
Janice and Lauren,
my husband, Allan,
and my parents, Lorna and Don

Table of Contents

Contents

Contents

Contents

Acknowledgments

For years, people have been telling me, "You have such great stories and so much wisdom; you should write a book." They made it sound easy: "Just let others into your mind, and the words will find their way." And you know, they were right! All I needed was an opportunity to share and the support and guidance of those who believed in me and my mission to help investors everywhere.

I am indebted to Jim Boyd, Executive Editor, and Russ Hall, Developmental Editor, Pearson Education, for recognizing the value of simple and straightforward advice. I owe thanks to my editors, Joelle Jay Ph.D., and Darrel Walters Ph.D., for helping me to organize my brain storms into practical prose. I am thankful to my many readers, particularly Lisa Goldenberg, who critiqued every word with steel cut precision.

Within Merrill Lynch, I enthusiastically acknowledge those mentors who have helped shape my vision of the financial advisory world: Larry Forlenza, David Komansky, and John "Launny" Steffens. I have had the outstanding support of Merrill Lynch management and communications, including John von Brachel, Selena Morris, Laura Townsend, Ted Durkin, Alan Wolf, and Paul Mullen. I offer special thanks to our new president, Sallie Krawcheck, who "gets it." It is a pleasure to have a leader whose values are so well aligned with the highest standards of the industry.

I have been privileged to work with the finest advisory team in the business, and I heartily thank my spectacular Merrill Lynch team: Johanna Walters, Megan Bailey, Krista Sheppard, Rose Zavasky, Gail Dontonville, Nichole Hilmer, and Beth Wagner. At home, I have been supported by my wonderful family, including my children, Janice and Lauren, my husband Allan, and my parents, Lorna and Don.

Finally, I thank the clients, who have been the greatest contributors to this learning process. I am appreciative of their trust and confidence and have been honored to serve them. While this book is to some degree about them, it is also *for* them, and I will always be grateful for the extraordinary relationships we have enjoyed together.

About the Author

Saly A. Glassman joined Merrill Lynch in 1980 after graduating from Cornell University, where she studied psychology. She was a leader in the early 1980s as one of the first financial consultants to advocate a total financial planning approach for clients.

Since 2004, when the *Barron's* Winner's Circle was initiated, Saly has been listed consistently among the 100 Top Best Financial Advisors and in the top three of the Women's Financial Advisors. Her advisory team has more than 135 years of collective experience and responsibility for over $2 billion of investments. Much of Saly's success stems from her "client-focused brand," a comprehensive financial services approach with retirement planning as a key component.

Saly is known for confidence in her principles and for skill in inspiring others to appreciate her point of view. She believes that financial well being encompasses personal health and the health of the community. An accomplished equestrian and avid cyclist, she developed a training and fitness center to help clients improve their wellness and quality of life. A strong proponent of conservation, Saly lives on a 128-acre preserved farm in Gwynedd Valley, Pennsylvania, with her husband, two daughters, and a multitude of dogs, cats, and horses.

Hello

In this introduction I'd like to talk with you briefly about your investments, your financial future, and your quality of life. That will prepare you to get the most out of this book.

In 29 years as a financial advisor with Merrill Lynch, I've seen enormous changes in the markets, the financial services industry, and even my own firm. A key objective of my professional career during those years has been to guide and educate clients. The downturn that began in mid-2007 has made me even more determined to use my experience to help simplify the investment process and offer practical advice that anyone would find valuable.

In the past you may have come to rely on what you considered conventional wisdom in your pursuit of successful investing. Perhaps as a result of this most recent crisis you have reconsidered what you thought it would take to achieve your goals. That would certainly be understandable. This particular market downturn has dealt such a devastating blow that everyone has been struck by it or knows someone who has. No one could blame you if you now wonder where this experience has left you and whose advice is safe to follow.

In my role as a financial advisor, I have talked at length with clients about their investment experiences. Like most people, you probably have lost money in one or more economic downturns. You may also have lost faith in the investment process. In this book, my primary goal is to help you get your investments back on track and restore the confidence you need to be a successful investor. Along the way, the insights I share will not only help you emerge victorious from the current financial crisis, but also prepare you to be a more successful investor in whatever markets lie ahead.

You may not think of yourself as an investor; however, if you have money that you want to protect and grow, you *are* an investor. You may have money in the bank, in bonds, in the stock market, in real estate, or in complex derivatives. That makes you more than just someone who has put aside a little money. You are not just a bank customer or a client of an investment brokerage firm. As long as you have saved money, you are making investments. You are an *investor,* and you need to take that role seriously.

How can you regain control of your financial life? First, you have to focus honestly and objectively on your past investment decisions and the consequences of your actions. Let's face it: For most investors, this is too great a responsibility to go it alone. For that reason, an important message throughout this book is that there may be distinct advantages in working with a financial advisor who is reliable and well suited to your circumstances.

Most likely you have at least one person functioning as an advisor already. Maybe your advisor is the account manager at your local bank or the person assigned to you when you walked into an investment firm. Maybe you obtained outside advice as to where to put your money. From whom did you accept advice? Was it your spouse? Your parents? Your friends? Any of these may be your advisor. Or you may have a financial advisor in the most traditional sense—a formal relationship with a qualified investment advisor at a bank, trust company, or investment brokerage firm.

You might be asking yourself, "Do I need to establish a formal relationship with a professional financial advisor to be considered the kind of "investor" for whom this book is written? The answer is "no." When I refer to investors in this book, I want you to know I'm talking to you. As an investor you deserve to be treated with care and respect, regardless of whether you use professional investment services. I want to acknowledge, however, the advantages of working with a professional financial advisor and selecting an advisor wisely. Whatever insight you gain here about how to think of investing and how to talk constructively to others about investing can help you make better investment decisions.

In the meantime, I will also guide you behind the scenes by offering insight into how to improve both your investment strategy and your overall financial picture. You'll be hearing true stories and quotes from actual investors. I have changed most names and supporting details to protect their privacy. You may find yourself having thoughts and opinions similar to theirs, or you may discover entirely new perspectives based on what they have to offer. The sharing of their dialogue may be just the ingredient you need to effectively evaluate your own actions.

One of my objectives in writing this book is to demystify the investment process so you, perhaps in league with your advisor, can develop and follow guidelines that will work for you. That is entirely possible even if you have little experience with investments. I intend to help you become empowered through knowledge and action-oriented practical advice.

Through this book I will be available to you every step of the way as you pursue success in your investments and in all your goals. Being successful relative to life's most important goals, after all, is about so much more than the money. Let's read on and learn more.

Chapter 1

Rules Are Essential, but They Do Not Guarantee a Win

Have you felt let down by an economic crisis? You might if you thought you were following all the investment rules you'd been taught. You may feel disappointed, resentful, and even angry. You are in good company if you are thinking, "I followed the rules! I should have won!" After all, doing so should entitle you to a certain reward. Doesn't following the rules protect you from losses, or at least minimize them?

Unfortunately, life doesn't work that way, and neither does the economy. Following investment rules doesn't necessarily mean you won't lose sometimes. However, using the rules as a general, meaningful guideline, even if you have to be flexible at times, is wise.

To succeed as an investor, you need to move beyond the emotional frustration of "losing" by examining your process and changing your behavior. This requires a constructive, focused, and objective mindset.

First, you have to acknowledge that there are no guarantees. But there are parameters to consider, and they are based on years of experience. Think of it this way. Picture a child running across the road between two parked cars on an active street. He makes it safely to the other side. He thinks, "Why do they tell me at school not to run between two parked cars? I did it, and nothing happened." Just because nothing happened one time doesn't mean it's a reasonable risk. One lucky win has nothing to do with the probability of future success. In fact, the probability of a win decreases with each risk taken because the odds will eventually catch up to you.

Yet sometimes this is how investors think. Either they have no investment rules, or they break their own rules and take on too much risk. When that rule-breaking strategy works, they do it again and again, thinking they are guaranteed phenomenal returns. Then they're surprised when they get run over!

The same scenario can also work the opposite way. An investor follows a rule, and it doesn't work. The investor "loses" and begins to think that following the rules doesn't matter because the rules can't guarantee safety. Think of a person who lives a healthy lifestyle, exercising and eating properly. She eats no fried food and avoids saturated fat. Can you guarantee that she won't get heart disease or cancer? No, but that doesn't mean that following the rules isn't a good idea. Although it may seem that the rules got her nowhere, the reality is they probably gained her a great deal. Could it be that her healthy eating prevented cancer from developing at an earlier date? Might she be more likely to beat heart disease because she is in great physical condition? Could it be that her quality of life before and during an illness could be improved by her healthy habits? Just as breaking the rules doesn't always lead to disaster, following the rules doesn't always lead to safety. That doesn't mean that following the rules is a bad idea.

When an economy turns south, many investors—including the ones who followed the rules—experience losses. This doesn't mean they should conclude they had poorly designed rules or that the rules don't work. Investment rules yield their effect over time. It's true that over short periods of time you might feel that you lost. You lost this one. You lost that one. But in the grand scheme of things, if you follow the rules—and we'll talk later about what those rule are—you're more likely to be on the right path.

Although you can't guarantee you'll never lose, what you can do is improve the probability of winning. That is what superior athletes do. Like the professional baseball player, all any of us can do is swing at the balls being pitched to us. And, like the baseball player, when you follow the right rules, you can increase your chances of getting a hit. You may not connect with the ball every time, but if you position your stance, practice your swing, and study the craft, the probability is that you are going to hit consistently over long periods of time. What do top players do to be in their best form? They study films, including those of the competition. They practice the skills they need until they are at the level of unconscious awareness. What looks like autopilot to us, the spectators, is really the result of years of active dedication to the sport. Top athletes are lifetime students of their game, and they learn to perform under pressure that includes less than desirable conditions. Will continual "perfect" practice always lead to a win? Is there a way to guarantee a connection with the ball? No. But practice greatly increases the chances of success. This reasoning applies to sports, investing, and anything else you value in your life.

Rules are guideposts that improve your probability, and that can make all the difference. What's the range, statistically speaking, between the minor leagues and the major leagues? For the best players, it can be very small. And yet, a ball player's life and the life of his family can be dramatically changed when he moves up to the major leagues and becomes a fixture there.

The same logic applies to the difference between mediocre and remarkable investment returns. From 1989 to early 2009, the Standard & Poor 500 stock market index return has been about 8.4% (J.P. Morgan Asset Management, *Guide to the Markets*, March 31, 2009). Can you guess what the average investor's rate of return has been over that period of time? About 2%. Why? Because investors, for whatever reasons, tend to buy high and sell low instead of doing the desired opposite. In any one year, the differential may not be that large. When you add all 20 years together, the cumulative effect is substantial.

Following are several ways you can improve the probability of "winning," which means increasing the potential for your investment performance.

Evaluate the Investment Rules You Followed

When you look back at the performance of your investments, ask yourself what rules you followed and how well they worked. Did you have the right rules? Were you following the rules that were appropriate for someone in your financial situation and at your stage of life? Did your situation change, and did that require revision to the rules?

This is how Rebecca describes her experience.

Rebecca: My husband and I were on a wonderful trip, hiking in Switzerland, when he suddenly had a heart attack and instantly died. I can't even describe the shock and pain of this; I was numb for weeks. When I got home, among all my new obligations I had the responsibility of all our investments, and I had never done any of this before. I discovered that there was quite a bit of money in higher risk securities. I learned to use a computer and I took a course on investing. I wanted to handle things personally, and before I knew it, I was day trading! I guess because my husband was an active trader, I thought that's what I was supposed to be doing. I was in over my head. I felt like there were no rules, or the rules that my husband had relied on previously were no longer appropriate for me, an inexperienced widow. I realized I needed an investment strategy with boundaries and an advocate to stand by me. It was a great relief when I found an advisor who was supportive and sensitive to my needs.

Examine How Well You Followed the Rules

It's painful to lose money. It especially hurts if you felt you were following the rules. But for the higher purpose of helping you to empower yourself, you need to look at yourself honestly. Did you *really* follow the rules? Did you follow them as closely as you could? Did you have a realistic time frame, or did you lose patience with the process? Maybe you had rules you weren't following at all. Maybe you were following other rules because you got distracted from the original rules you established.

Charles talks about how this happened to him.

Charles: For 20 years I have had a successful business in home security systems. I am confident and have a strong head for financial decisions. I always believed in diversification and therefore used different asset classes. This meant being invested in stocks, bonds, real estate, even art and collectibles. Each time I had a positive investment result, I added more money to that specific category because I was so pleased with how things were working out. Eventually, I had large sums deployed in more aggressive and illiquid assets, and the returns took a negative shift. I kept telling myself that these things just needed more time, but I ultimately had to acknowledge that I lost track of my own rules for managing risk. I was attracted to the high potential returns and forgot to limit the percentage of funds in each asset class.

Get Back in the Game

To paraphrase Yogi Berra, the game isn't over until it's over. You may have temporarily lost money, maybe even a lot of it. But as long as you're an investor committed to your future, you still have the opportunity to participate constructively as the market recovers. You have options.

You can improve how you're handling your investments. One of the ways you surmount a crisis is to remember that you can be a strong force in your financial recovery if you can step away for a minute to examine your game. What investments should you be in now? Are you in them? Addressing your investment strategy is one way to correct the mistakes of the past and position yourself better for the future.

You can cut your expenses. When you go through a financial crisis, suddenly you become an expert on what you must have versus what you can live without. Can you do some of the things you used to pay others to do and do those things just as well? Can you cut expenses without significantly reducing your quality of life?

You can add to your income. You may go back to work or earn some extra money by doing something for which you have unique expertise. You can sell things of value, like furniture or jewelry. You may love to have nice things, but can you live without them? Do you have any valuable objects you thought meant something to you and now you realize their intrinsic value has decreased? Perhaps now you can trade for cash and buy some time while you get stabilized.

You can prioritize your life. Maybe you lost some money in the financial markets, but did you lose in every game you were playing? Maybe you are focusing on one game that you lost, but maybe you won a lot of others. How satisfying is your family life? How rewarding are your friendships? How's your health? To move past the anger of losing, it helps to step back and view the broad canvas of your life. Money isn't the entire puzzle; it's only one piece! Look again at what you thought you wanted. Ask yourself, "Is that still how I feel, or have my priorities changed?" Maybe what you thought you wanted isn't really what you wanted, or maybe you can achieve those same things in another way.

Here is Dan's story:

Dan: I retired with what I thought was a lot of money, and I had big plans to dabble in real estate and enjoy my avocations, which are very expensive pastimes. In this most recent crisis, my liquid assets and real estate plummeted, and my expenses went up! I was so stressed out about paying my bills that my hobbies no longer provided me with satisfaction. In fact, because of their expense, they were compounding my anxiety. I had to go back to square one and evaluate my life. I realized that my heart just wasn't in these high-powered activities any more, and I was actually relieved when I successfully abandoned them in favor of more volunteer work and time spent with my family. This change helped me get my finances under control and simplify my life. Even though this was a difficult experience, I consider it a win.

The score is about more than what happens when you're standing at home plate. When you're at the plate, all you can think about is getting a hit, maybe even a home run. But there's a bigger picture: what your fans are thinking about you, how valuable you are to your team, what kind of example you are to the sport, what kind of a student you are of the game, and how much you are enjoying winning. The end game is about so much more than that one big hit.

If you follow the right rules, you'll ultimately be a winner. You may win in a way that is far more important than the way you used to keep score. In adverse circumstances, when it feels that you're losing, losing, losing, you can start to feel like a loser. It's only when you lose the little stuff that you realize you may have been winning in a big way all along. You may also discover the potential to "win" in a way you had not previously considered. Develop rules that make sense for you and follow them. Give them time to work and reevaluate them when necessary. In the long run, following the right rules will bring you closer to winning.

Chapter 2

Focus Your Predictions on What You Can Control: Your Priorities

Predictions are part of investing, and yet they are frequently misapplied or misunderstood. What purpose do predictions serve? How do predictions help us to make better decisions?

History—the past—is something we know with some certainty. But there's an ever present mystery about what's ahead. No one knows what's going to happen in the future. We can make assumptions. We can speculate. We can guess. But ultimately, we all have to admit that we're not clairvoyant; we can't foretell the future. What we can do is study the past, identify patterns, and then apply the knowledge of patterns to the present. Still, our financial planning will be built more solidly on personal goals than on predictions dictated by history.

At certain times, predictions make sense. For example, if you leave a piece of unprotected steel exposed to the elements for an extended period, you can expect it to rust. That's a safe prediction, so you'll want to paint the steel or protect it in some other way to avoid the rust. Because your prediction of rust is based on scientific evidence, there's a strong likelihood it will be accurate.

That kind of predictability goes out the window in contexts having less consistency than steel + moisture + time + oxygen = rust. The financial market is just such a context, buffeted as it is by a host of variables. There's what's happening with investors...with a company...the international markets...the direction of interest rates... where the economy is going...the political environment. Various shifting factors influence our ability to make predictions.

When you think about all these variables, you may ask yourself, "Do predictions have any validity at all?" They do, but they need to be informed predictions based on factors over which you have some control.

Predictions need to be seen for what they are. They are a series of carefully calculated assumptions based on patterns of the past. They are one piece of what goes into the investment planning process. The other components are also important, such as having an asset allocation strategy, managing risk, actively saving, having reasonable goals and expectations for market returns, and reviewing performance.

No matter how well you feel you can make predictions, you cannot be certain. Even an informed advisor can't be sure because investing involves continual oncoming blind curves. Advisors can't see around those curves any more than you can. It's unrealistic to expect that they can. What advisors can do is apply their experience with blind curves to new events. They have been down this road or one like it previously, possibly hundreds of times, so their level of familiarity is likely to be higher. People who have studied the financial markets for many years have learned to recognize and take note of patterns. Even though history does not repeat itself, as Mark Twain said, "it rhymes." So the patterns have similarities. For example, we can pinpoint moments of irrational exuberance, such as in late 1999 during the Internet craze. We can also highlight moments of deep depression and hopelessness, such as the stock market trough of October, 2002. In short, the experience financial advisors have with patterns gives them a context to work with—a context that makes the unfamiliar appear, to some extent, familiar.

An advisor can study developing trends, identify trends that are in place, and make assumptions about the potential longevity of each trend based on history, science, and mathematical probability. As these trends age, an advisor can estimate the risks involved in continuing to participate in the trend and make adjustments for the inevitable new trends that lie ahead. But remember, all the information we have about market trends is based on only 100 years of history. The stock market was not started until the early 20th century, and so all the possible blind curves have not had time to reveal themselves. There are more to come!

You can accomplish a great deal by making predictions based on reliable information. It's when there's a clairvoyant component that predictions become unreliable. An advisor's crystal ball has plenty of cracks and clouds, just as yours does! Questions like, "What do you think the market's going to do?" and "What do you think the Federal Reserve will do with interest rates?" are far from the scientific element. The answers tend to be unreliable because they're based on variables over which you have no control.

When it comes to your investments, you need to make the right kinds of predictions—using tools based on historical patterns, scientific evidence, and mathematic probability. Even then, you need to make those predictions with reasonable expectations. In other words, you can't rely on predictions alone to make financial decisions. You need an investment strategy with a contingency plan built in.

Here is an exercise to consider: Imagine what a portfolio might look like with an investor's goals ranked as follows:

- Financial security
- Family
- Health
- Hobbies
- Career

That's Person One. Now let's look at another person's list.

- Career
- Hobbies

- Financial Security
- Family
- Health

That's Person Two. Do you see how these two people might have two substantially different investment strategies?

Look at Person One first. If financial security comes first, what is she going to be most concerned with regarding her money? Not losing it! If family comes next, she's going to want to have a family estate plan in place. If health is third, perhaps it's of some importance, but she might skip some health related steps if she's worried about spending too much money. (Remember, in her priorities, financial security comes first.) Hobbies were last, so although she probably has some enjoyable activities, if she had to live without them she could. She may also be putting the hobbies of other family members ahead of her own interests. Her financial strategy needs to reflect her priorities.

Now let's look at Person Two. His first priority is his career. At the start of each day, his first thoughts might be about how to get ahead, increase his compensation, get more notoriety, or receive credit for his accomplishments. He may feel he can invest with some degree of abandonment because his career is being launched successfully, and he doesn't need any income from his investments. For this person, hobbies are the second priority. He works hard and plays hard. Financial security is the third priority. Maybe this person realizes that he can't work forever, so he decides to save a little money. Nevertheless, because of the way he's ranked his priorities, he's not giving up his hobbies, and it doesn't matter if those hobbies jeopardize his security a little bit because his hobbies are a higher priority than financial security. Family comes fourth. Because his career comes first, he might not give a lot of thought to family life. This is a very different profile than our first example, Person One.

Focus Your Predictions on What You Can Control: Your Priorities

It can be enlightening to do the following exercise with your spouse and with adult children who would like to participate in the process. Give everyone 20 seconds to write spontaneous answers to some questions. Warm them up first with a few fun and random questions, such as:

- What are your favorite colors?
- What are your favorite birds?
- What is the best month of the year?
- What is your favorite time of day?

Limit everyone to 5 to 10 seconds for their responses. When they have the hang of it, ask them this question:

- What are your most important priorities, in ranked order?

Have them rank their priorities. If they need prompting, offer them suggestions as to what they might include:

- Financial security
- Family
- Health
- Hobbies
- Career
- Philanthropy/charity
- Religion/spirituality

Here's where it gets complicated. When everyone writes down an answer, the next question is the most interesting:

- Is that what you are living?

The answer is not always yes. This is a critical lesson to apply to your investment strategies, which may be misaligned with your priorities.

After you rank your priorities from a financial perspective, you can start taking some control over the way you handle your investments. What if health is one of your priorities? What actions are you taking with your own resources to get yourself in the best health? Are you exercising frequently? Are you a regular participant at a gym? Do you maintain a healthy diet? Do you know the details of your health insurance, such as the terms of your co-pay and quality of services? Have you made a commitment to your physical well-being, and is health care an integral part of your life?

From a career standpoint, does your career offer strong financial potential? Are you focused on how you can enhance your levels of achievement?

In your family, are your children being well educated? Are their emotional needs being met? Are they going to summer camp? Do they have expensive hobbies? Are they going to college, and are you going to pay for it? Are they planning to intern in the family business in preparation for a career there?

As you consider your priorities, you are making financial connections, discovering what actions you should take and how your investment strategy should be refined. As a result, your strategy will be based on what's important to you. Any predictions you make are related to what's true about you—and your strategy is based on so much more than just predictions.

Your investments should serve the higher purpose of getting you as close as possible to your most important goals. Therefore, you need to be connected to your investments. You can design an investment strategy only after you know what's important to you—your highest priorities.

You can't predict what you can't control. So don't make all your investment decisions based on predictions. Make them by having an investment strategy based on your true priorities. Ironically, after you integrate your priorities into the mix, your investments will have a much higher probability of being successfully predicted!

In case something unexpected should happen, you also need to have a contingency plan. What would you do if things did not go the way you expected? Let's say you rank your career first on your list of priorities, indicating that your career is of the greatest importance to you. You've invested heavily in your career and made a long-term commitment to it. Because career is high up on the list, you're relying on the income it generates to drive your investment strategy. But what if something happened and you lost your job or were injured? In that case, your career would be unable to fulfill that role, and your investment strategy would have to rely on your other priorities.

You have options at this point. You might accumulate enough money to prepare in advance for this event. You might have adequate health, life, and disability insurance. These are only a couple of the strategies that contribute to a well-designed contingency plan.

When you have a solid contingency plan guarding your priorities, your ability to predict your future has an added boost of support. When something goes wrong, you don't have to stop and think about how to handle it. You rely confidently on your contingency plan and make very quick adjustments.

One investor, Brian, had personal experience with this.

Saly: What kind of a contingency plan did you have when you first contemplated retiring, and how has it worked for you?

Brian: I worked in sales in the grocery business for many years. I've always enjoyed my work. It's not that I wanted to retire. I just wanted to take it easy a little bit. I always thought my profession was recession-resistant. People have always needed food! As I began to downsize my business activity, my advisor reminded me that I needed to put some additional cash aside just in case my income would fall unexpectedly because I wasn't putting the same effort into my work that I once was. At the time I remember thinking that this seemed overly conservative, even gloomy. I wondered if it was even necessary. After all, it wasn't like I was quitting. Then this most recent economic downturn came around, and I have to admit, sales fell off. I started to wonder if I could even keep the work I had been doing, even though it was scaled down. I was concerned that my job might actually be eliminated. I realized that having an emergency fund was a great idea. Although I never needed to tap my investments, it was a great feeling knowing the funds were there. As it turned out my business didn't suffer in a major way. The market change and my concerns were temporary. I never really felt the pressure that my friends have who are my age and still working. I think it's because I had a cash cushion and they didn't.

To summarize, you can't predict what you can't control. You can make some predictions, and an informed advisor can help you make even better decisions. But it's unrealistic to rely solely on predictions as an investment strategy. A more reasonable approach is to design an investment strategy around your ranked priorities, with a contingency plan to back it up.

Chapter 3

Let Go of What Might Have Been

You are no doubt familiar with phrases like

- I would have…
- I could have…
- I should have…
- I might have…
- I wish that…
- If only…

Phrases like these have their own special ring. They're a way to absolve yourself from your original planning and expectations, and at the same time they are a form of self-sabotage that prevents you from moving forward in a productive way.

There is a difference between learning constructive lessons from your experiences and dwelling on the past. Focusing on "what might have been" can be an unproductive and painful process. The use of this sort of thinking is revealing in that it shows we are (1) critiquing ourselves after the fact, (2) expressing discomfort with the choices we made, and possibly (3) looking for ways to deflect our own responsibility and accountability. You will do better to forget this as a way of viewing your financial life and practice a more constructive approach. This can be achieved in three steps.

Step 1: Learn to Recognize the "What Might Have Been" in Your Language

When you become aware of this language, you can become more conscious of the way you use it. The "what might have been" has a way of punishing you for the past, including the parts of the past that were out of your control. You might say, for example, "I had a feeling that the market was going to go down. I should have sold my stocks." Does that mean that in your investment strategy and your original asset allocation you were too aggressive to begin with? Does it mean you lost your focus and weren't paying attention when your asset allocation rules got violated? Did you change your standards midstream and invest in products that weren't part of your original investment strategy, and now you're angry with yourself? Did you have unreasonable expectations? Did you think the market would go up 20% year after year after year, and would do that especially for you even if it didn't do that for anyone else?

Can you see how this kind of "what might have been" thinking works against you? When you hear yourself thinking or speaking this way, acknowledge the fact that it has worked its way into your language. Look at why it's there and question its usefulness. Ask yourself, "Where am I going with this line of thinking? Why am I using this kind of language? Where is this type of thinking going to lead me?"

The "what might have been" is "Monday morning quarterbacking" at its finest. It's taking the information you have now, after all the events have occurred, and critiquing the decisions you made before you had that information. No amount of this kind of analysis is going to change the outcome. Look at it this way. At the time you made the decisions, were they the right decisions based on the information you had then? Give yourself some credit! If you made the best decisions with the advice and knowledge you had at the time, there's no point in flogging yourself because events went differently and you didn't get the results you wanted.

When you catch yourself using this kind of self-talk, ask yourself, "What purpose does this language serve?"

Step 2: See It for What It Really Is

The "what might have been" view of investing (and, frankly, everything) does not take you closer to solving your problems. It allows you to escape from them.

One way people use the "what might have been" is to blame themselves. In what follows, a retired investor, Gretchen, talks about how she and her friends have used this way of thinking to blame themselves for money they lost in the recent economic crisis.

Saly: What errors have your friends made through this crisis? Do they talk about their mistakes and how they are adjusting? Do they reveal what they're doing differently now?

Gretchen: They talk about all the money they lost, and considering we are all from this generation, we are very, very upset. We have worked so hard for it. None of it has been given to us. It's like taking a match and burning a stack of $20 bills, which none of us would ever do. Even our wealthiest friends can't figure out what they did wrong, and they still don't know how to get out of this predicament. However, our lives have not changed that much because we chose to wait things out. We kid around and say we should have bought that house on the beach like someone told us to do. But this time even the ones who are knowledgeable in the market got hurt. Should have, could have, would have. You know, hindsight is perfect! I'm also one of those people who looks back and says, "If only."

Saly: Why do you look back and second guess yourself?

Gretchen: Fear of what's going to happen in the future and regret over why I didn't do this or that. Why wasn't I paying more attention? Why wasn't I more knowledgeable? Why did I put my faith in other people? Why can't I be smarter?

You can hear in this conversation that Gretchen and her friends use the "what might have been" to review what's happened to them financially in the recent year. Can you also hear her sense of anger, loss, and regret? This is very disempowering. It's as if your alter ego is saying, "You fool. It was perfectly obvious that you should have done that thing, and instead you chose the other thing." How can this thinking lead to constructive solutions? It doesn't.

In addition to blaming themselves, investors use the "what might have been" to blame others. Instead of saying "I should have...." they say, *"You should have...."* When investors do this, they are deflecting responsibility from themselves and onto someone else.

Both investors and advisors can fall into this trap. The message seems to be, "If you should have done something differently, then I'm innocent. I was just sitting here waiting and watching and being the investor or the advisor." From the advisor's point of view, the language might sound like this: "You should have modified your lifestyle. Look at how you were living. In spite of everything I advised, you were spending excessively and acting as if you would never run out of money. You should have changed your behavior." From the investor's position, it might sound like this: "You should have stopped me! You didn't say anything! You saw the checks I wrote, but you didn't intervene. You just let me spend! Where were you when I needed you?" Investors and advisors can end up pointing fingers at each other, and meanwhile the problems don't get solved.

Instead of starting the phrase with *you* should have or even *I* should have, make a commitment to look at things in a completely new way.

Step 3: Eliminate the "What Might Have Been" from Your Language

Notice What Factors Are and Are Not in Your Control

The "what might have been" may be a natural reaction to circumstances, but it is also often irrational, especially when you use it to blame yourself for factors out of your control. In the game of roulette, when you've selected red and then black wins, you might say, "Oh! I was going to pick black!" And then you realize that's ridiculous because roulette is a game of chance. What good does it do to examine your performance in a game you have no control over winning?

When things don't work out in your favor, remember that some events were completely out of your control. Then you can focus on the parts you can control for a more productive outcome the next time. Jordan, an executive coach and investor, shares her perspective:

Saly: If your advisor gave you advice that perhaps didn't work well, or you were disappointed with your investment performance, what would you do?

Jordan: I would be constructively confrontational. If it were a big deal, I would come in to speak in person. I would be straightforward and put my cards on the table. I would say, this is how I feel about X. Let's revisit the situation to see if there's anything that we should have done differently or that we can change now. All my future money, everything I have, is contingent upon our supportive relationship and our ability to work together. Before I would ever change my advisor, I would have to commit to some extensive soul searching to find out what's wrong in this relationship. What accountability did I have? What accountability did my advisor have? How would a new relationship compare with my existing one?

Jordan already has a plan for the potential of an undesirable situation. She knows to look for factors she can influence or control, analyze them honestly, and take responsibility for her own conduct.

Learn from Your Mistakes and Change for the Next Time

Instead of talking about what could have, would have, or should have happened, talk about what did happen and what you want to have happen in the future. Use the past tense. ("I did this, and you did that. We did this.") Now look at how effective these actions were. ("We did this, and it had this result. We did that, and it had that result. Are we happy with what we did? No. So what will we do in the future?") Finally, go to the future tense. ("We will do this in the future. I will do this, and you will do that. We agree on what we will do.") Then you can implement your strategy. When we take this more constructive line of thinking, we make present what we want for the future because, of course, the future begins now. When the advisor and client accept responsibility for the past, present, and future, there is no longer any purpose for the subjunctive. This kind of thinking applies even if you do not have a formal advisory relationship.

Renee provides an example of how she has used her past experiences to reconcile her former "what might have been" self in the following discussion. Renee grew up in an affluent household from generations of inherited wealth. During her adolescence and early adulthood, her immediate family's extravagant lifestyle led to these assets being greatly depleted. Renee was left with a much smaller investment portfolio as a result, and she had to learn to adjust to her new reality.

Renee: If you have a lesson, learn it and keep it with you for the rest of your life. That's what made the biggest impression on me. I grew up in a house with extraordinary wealth and all that anyone could dream of. One of the things I discovered pretty quickly was that money didn't provide the love and attention that children long for, so I was always happier at other people's houses than I was at my own. I would have given all the money back in exchange for a happy childhood.

I do think about the fact that I spent quite a bit of money during a period when money was accessible, but I don't allow myself to dwell on it because that also was a lesson. I refuse to feel bad about it because I had some incredible experiences and a lot of fun. I've been places a lot of people have never been, and I consider that to be a gift to myself. But I'm very proud of the fact that when my advisor cracked the whip and said enough is enough, I said okay because if you have the right values you can do away with all the fluff. It was a harsh moment when I realized that I could not depend on what "should have been" mine, and I have had to rely on myself, financially and personally, from that point on. I had to grow up.

When you avoid the "what might have been," you learn from your mistakes!

Take Full Responsibility

The "what might have been" perspective makes you the victim. It's a protective mechanism. If you are weak, you need to berate yourself— or perhaps blame someone else so you can avoid accountability. That's very disempowering. As an investor, you can gain power by taking full responsibility for your own decisions, which puts you back in control. Listen to the way Estelle, an investor in her late 40s, talks about this mindset.

> **Estelle**: My husband and I are two people who are really rooted in the belief that "If you're going to make it happen, it starts with you." If we had lost all our money in the recent downturn, we would have been devastated. But we knew full well that ultimately it was up to us to stay on top of what was going on, to make decisions, get advice, and move things around. There are a lot of people who talk about "should have, could have, would have."

> I remember two years ago we wanted to put more money in stocks, and our advisor said, "Your asset allocation is already well represented in stocks, and I am against a strategy change that increases your short-term risk." It was my responsibility to take that advice or not. I stepped back and asked myself, "What do you have the money for?" That helped me to understand and accept my advisor's reasoning. I want to pay my bills. I want to feel good that I can hold my head high as an upstanding citizen. I want to get my kids through college, but beyond that I don't want to die with it and I certainly don't want the government to get it all. There's a balance there. You never know what's ahead and what you might need later.

It's inspirational to say, "I studied my behavior, I made changes, and I'm doing things differently now. I acknowledge my mistakes, and I will do this from now on. I'm in charge, and I am on my way to a more responsible and self-driven perspective."

True, the "what might have been" can play a role in the short term. It feels good. It's like biting your nails: It works for a little while to help you deal with anxiety, but it doesn't solve any problems. In fact, it causes more problems. Habits like nail biting—and the "what might have been"—can be very hard to break. If you want to make progress as an investor and an advisor, take that first step and refuse to use it in your language. You'll be confronted with what's left, which is you, your responsibility, and your accountability. Can that be hard to accept? Yes. But it's also the way to succeed as an investor.

Let's summarize the steps:

1. Watch for situations where you may be inadvertently sabotaging yourself.
2. Acknowledge your mistakes and learn from them.
3. Change your behavior.
4. Have a contingency plan for what you're going to do when things don't go the way you intended.
5. When you catch yourself using the "what might have been," stop and ask, "What do I really mean? Do I mean that I should have planned more thoroughly and paid closer attention? What's my role in the decisions that I made?"

You can avoid the "what might have been" and find a more productive way to think. When you find it, that's when you will discover the path to real growth, personally and financially.

Chapter 4

Take Responsibility

"I am so sick of Wall Street and all the money those people made."

"I have to blame the regulators. They didn't protect us when we were relying on them."

"I can't believe what happened in the mortgage market with subprime loans and the extent of indiscriminate lending."

"I'm really angry. I feel let down by the system."

"I'm disappointed because I feel like there's no one I can trust."

Comments like these from investors reflect feelings of pain and betrayal. In a depressed economy, it may seem quite understandable. You may even know how they feel.

Let's look at the collective tone of these remarks. All these comments from investors focus on blaming another party to justify their feelings. That's one approach to responding to an economic downturn. But it's not the only option. When it comes to our own investing, we have a choice to make. We can either take the path of blame and put the responsibility for our circumstances onto everyone else, or we can accept accountability for ourselves. Let's look at each option.

Option 1: Blame Others

Option one is to take no responsibility. That's a position of weakness, no matter how strong you feel while you're placing the blame. If you take no responsibility, you're automatically disengaged from your economic circumstance. "I had nothing to do with it! I'm just a victim!"

you say. Listen to how this approach sounds in the words of an investor named Valerie.

> **Valerie:** I didn't really watch the market every day. I just assumed that over the long term, things would go up, and if they went down, it wouldn't be that dramatic. Suddenly, overnight, I felt punched in the gut. I had to totally remake the way I thought about my life—my spending, my investments, what's important to me. For the first time ever, I remember being really nervous about my future. I had saved all this money. I thought I was conservative. I might as well have just had a big party and spent it all. At least I would have had a great time for one night!

This is a hopeless thinking pattern. "Why did I save and do all these things so carefully?" Valerie asks. But how does that line of thought help Valerie triumph over this tough situation? It doesn't. When you choose to be the victim, you automatically disengage yourself from participating in the solution. That's a choice. It may feel comforting to be a victim while you're wallowing in it, but ultimately it doesn't do anything for you except delay your ability to recover.

If you don't take responsibility as an investor, you essentially just let things happen to you. You don't fairly acknowledge any kind of role that you might have had. There are other problems with not taking responsibility.

- You don't learn anything from the experience, so you can't teach the lessons to yourself, your children, or other people you care about.
- You prevent yourself from being part of the solution.
- You can't learn from your mistakes.
- You may harbor bitterness and resentment.

Blame is not a solution. It stems from our desire to attribute negative experiences to someone else's actions. Then we don't have to face reality. We don't have to recognize that we should have saved more or should have done more research on a product or a person. Maybe we should have waited, or not waited.

Not taking responsibility ultimately works against you. How do you reverse the pattern and get away from this blaming mindset? Let's look at the positives of what happens when you do take responsibility.

Option 2: Take Responsibility

The first step to taking responsibility is to accept your participation in the process.

The hard reality is this: We all played a part in the market upswing that preceded the economic downturn of recent years. Every one of us participated in some way, and it's almost cavalier to pretend that as horrible things were happening all around us, we had nothing to do with them. Every investor was a part of the economic good time, and we have to admit that we either initiated or benefited by events in some way.

If investors associated with Wall Street made a lot of money, it's because the stock market went up. If the stock market went up and you had investments, you made money as your investments appreciated. If you refinanced your mortgage quickly and easily with little need for documentation, it's because mortgage refinancing was administratively simple and credit standards were lax. Perhaps you sold a business for a large sum of money and the buyer financed it with debt that was unsecured. That sale may have been easier because of the availability of that debt, and you got the cash. In addition, you may have had a favorable tax rate on your capital gain.

The first step in taking responsibility is to assess the role you personally played in the whole cascade of events that occurred and acknowledge how you participated. That doesn't mean you may not still be mad at everybody else! But when you can see the part you've played in the economy—either by initiating, participating, or benefiting—you can consider whether you're ready to take responsibility for that role so that you can get back to winning.

Marvin talks about how he was enticed by a variety of investment opportunities. Although he was initially inclined to blame someone else, ultimately he accepted responsibility for his actions.

> **Marvin:** From the very first moment I met my new advisors I was "sold." You know what they say. It's easy to sell to a salesman. For example, when I went to the investment firm, I had days—literally, days!—where I was bombarded by every different type of esoteric investment they had. I met the vice chairman of this group and the senior vice president of that group and the managing director of this group and had all these intensive meetings. They could have sold me the Brooklyn Bridge after 5 days, and I didn't have a clue as to what they were talking about. I was dealing with the hierarchy of one of the top firms. I guess I always wanted to be on the inside. I always thought that Wall Street guys made a lot of money because of this. They had access to deals that people on the outside didn't have. And boy, after those 5 days, I was shown situations that a normal investor would never have seen. You name it; they had it. And I never understood whom I was hiring or what I was buying.

That's a pretty scary scenario. Marvin also made another important point.

> **Marvin:** I learned my lesson. I am not going to change as a human being. I am very trustworthy, and I'm trusting. I've been burned, and I'm not the only one in the world who's been in this position. You ultimately have to go with your instincts. Sometimes you're going to be right, and sometimes

you're going to be wrong. Because I am a person who is inclined to be trusting, I realize that I must do my research up front at the beginning of my relationships so that I make the right choices early on and don't regret my actions later.

When you take responsibility as an investor, you have the opportunity to fairly reevaluate what's happened and reposition for greater success. You're less likely to repeat mistakes. You're a better role model and example to others. You can be proud of your courage and development as a person. You can find leverage. You can exert influence toward improving the quality of regulation. You can clear the way for the next investor. That next person could be someone you really care about, like one of your own children. Even when you've suffered losses and disappointments, there's more to be gained by taking responsibility than by placing blame.

So how do you begin? To fully take responsibility for your investments, you need a master plan for your life.

A Master Plan for Your Life

In Chapter 2, "Focus Your Predictions on What You Can Control: Your Priorities," we talked about the importance of knowing your priorities. Those priorities are stepping stones to the global master plan you have for your life.

When you take responsibility as far as you can in every aspect of your life—with your health, your family, your education—the possibilities are endless as to what you can accomplish. When it comes to investments, the first step is to examine the whole picture for the master plan for your life. What's important to you, and how are you going to get it? The idea is that if you can see a vision for that master plan, you can begin to orchestrate with higher confidence the components that go into it. You create the plan in stages.

Get the Bigger Picture for Your Life

Your master plan starts with your overall vision—a view of your life from 20,000 feet. In general, what do you want? Think of all the choices you can make about your job, home, family, vacations, hobbies, and health, and how you will get the most out of your life. What is most important to you?

Look at the Path from Where You Are Now to Where You Want to Be

The path for many people involves a gradual transition from human capital to financial capital over time. When you're younger, you use your skills to make money. What you're doing is using yourself to get leverage. This is what we call human capital. It creates the funds you can invest and then grow. Investing is about the transition of human capital to financial capital over long periods of time. You build up additional assets through your investments, and eventually if you have a well-thought-out master plan, you can make the transition from human capital (working) to financial capital (retirement, not working, working less, or doing something different).

As you create the master plan for your life, think about what this transition would look like for you. You can look at the accomplishments generated by your human capital and appreciate how it will be expanded, leveraged, and then harvested, so you can have financial assets that will ultimately replace your human capital.

It's then your responsibility to fulfill all the components that drive the transition. This includes hiring the advisor, learning about investments, saving enough money, having the right time frame, developing a reasonable asset allocation, monitoring, and evaluating progress, holding people accountable, and ultimately being able to make that transition.

Map Out a Strategy

When you have the bigger picture of your life in mind and a sense of how you will move from human to financial capital over time, then it's time to map out a strategy based on your goals, resources, risk tolerance, and the timeline. Here's how it looks. You approach your advisor and say, "This is what I want in my life." Then you discuss your goals and resources with your advisor. Elements might include

- Your profession
- Your income
- Your time frame
- Your priorities
- Other financial hopes (such as college tuition, travel, a house at the seashore, and so on) and a sense of what they cost

Now your advisor knows what you want and has learned more about what you can contribute to the picture. Together, you and your advisor can design a strategy that uses what you have to create what you want. This involves discussion about the time frame, your risk temperament, and the investment strategy that would be necessary to accomplish the goal.

Unfortunately, this is where a lot of strategies break down. Sometimes investors don't want to face the reality of what's possible given what they have, what they want, their time frame, and their goals. Here, the advisor can help them to establish more realistic expectations. On the other hand, if the advisor does think the goals are reasonable, the next step is to work out the details that will have the highest probability of making that investment strategy a success.

Take Responsibility for the Master Plan

At this point, you have in mind your vision, your path to the vision, and a strategy for succeeding along that path. This is your master plan. Now you need to take responsibility for monitoring it. How frequently are you going to be communicating about how well the strategy is doing? What steps are you going to take to help when the strategy goes the wrong way because markets are not as accommodating as they may have been in the past? How will you handle changes in your career, health, and family needs?

When you take responsibility as an investor, you empower yourself to turn your master plan into reality. On the day when you decide to harvest your accumulated assets and transition from human capital to financial capital, you can look back and survey everything that you've accomplished. And although you may acknowledge that you've made some mistakes, you can be proud of what you've done because *you've* done it. You didn't just drift down the river in a little basket. You took command of your ship and crossed a vast ocean.

Chapter 5

Do What You Know and Recognize What You Don't Know

One of the strongest pieces of advice I can give an investor is to *do what you know*. To illustrate this, I'd like to share a cautionary tale about what happens when you don't. Meet Jake.

Jake: I used to be interested in a lot of different aspects of boating, and I had some friends—also orthopedic surgeons, like me—who shared that interest. One of them approached me and suggested I participate with five other physicians in forming a small company. This guy's brother owned a marina in South Carolina and talked a good game. The whole idea was that a radical design had been created by a very famous naval architect. It was a high-speed fishing boat with a special kind of hull that would make the boat faster and more stable. It would cost a certain amount of money to buy the mold and transport it to South Carolina, where there are boat-making operations. We could create the design, and then we could sell these boats very easily because they were unique.

Through a couple of meetings, he convinced us each to invest $250,000 to develop the company and market the boats. He shared a business plan with lots of glossy pictures and projected revenue streams. Looking back on it, of course, it was all pie-in-the-sky stuff, but it was based on numbers and potential sales, and there were all these connections with high-powered people.

We called our financial advisor, who had a negative reaction. We were advised, "This is a business with which you are not familiar. You should be doing what you do best, which is surgery. This will be a distraction. It's highly speculative and could jeopardize your financial security. If you absolutely feel you must participate, do it with a small amount of money: less than $50,000.

But gosh, there was a lot of social pressure, and it looked so enticing! We ended up putting $250,000 in against our advisor's advice.

At this time interest rates were fairly low, so on the advice of one of the other participants, we got a second mortgage with an adjustable interest rate, and borrowed $200,000. We used $50,000 in cash from our investment account.

We met every couple weeks in a small factory to see how things were progressing. In the beginning, it did seem that there was a reasonable plan; we were all like-minded. With the special mold for the hull, it was clear the boat would be faster, stronger, lighter, and more fuel efficient. This was all part of the sales pitch.

The fatal flaw that we made, which of course now we realize—and it seems so simple, I don't know what we were thinking!—we didn't do background checks on these people. How could we have missed that step? When I think of all the times people come to me for medical advice, of course, they looked me up and read something about me. It's so simple, and I just didn't do it. And of course, the second mistake we made was not taking the advice of our advisor to at least minimize the risk levels. What we did do was tell the group, "This is all you're getting from us; we're not putting any more money into this later." However, that also became an issue, as I'll tell you about in a minute.

We started meeting every 2 to 3 weeks in this production facility. It was taking a long time to build just one boat, and there was always a need for more cash to improve the design or acquire supplies.

After 3 to 4 months, I thought, "Wow, I don't get this. We're spending all this money, and we're selling a boat for less than what it costs to make." We were told that the supplies had to be shipped in. The production crews were transient, which led to a lot of turnover. It became apparent that we didn't really have a clue what was going on. We had no control over where money was going. There was pressure to put more money up, despite our original commitment to the contrary. We needed diesel engines; we needed hardware. As it all began to come apart, we realized that we had made a terrible mistake.

We knew then that we had to get out of this situation. A rift developed because half the group wanted to exit the deal, and half of the group wanted to continue. It began to feel like extortion. The message was, "If you don't put money in, this project is going to fail, and we're all going to lose our money." There was pressure for us to continue investing, but the boats weren't being produced.

Ultimately, we ended up in a spectacular lawsuit to extricate ourselves from the whole experience. The lesson we learned is that even if you're passionate about something and have an interest in a business enterprise, unless you have a business background, don't do it without professional advice. We did have an accountant, but the accountant was more of a bill payer, not a boat-building consultant. We should have taken our financial advisor's advice and recognized that this venture was far out of our expertise, and there was way too much risk. We ended up in a hostile, vindictive game. We had to spend exorbitant legal costs on top of what we had invested just to get ourselves out from under. We had vendors coming after us, and we had acrimonious phone calls and meetings. Luckily, our advisor connected us with assertive legal professionals, who helped us to avoid bankruptcy.

The experience has made me more cautious about decisions I make now. I recognize I need to look at a business plan, the market, the risk, and the exit strategy—something I never considered. I was foolish to take all that on without having legal counsel to review the documents. I was naïve about the industry, and I was blinded to the market forces that were shifting. Just because you like wearing shoes doesn't mean you can make them.

The odd and disturbing thing is that I don't have the same feeling for boating I once had. It soured my feelings in some ways—even a little bit about the marina and the lifestyle I had once loved. I'll tell you something else. I think that doing business with friends is a recipe for disaster. We told our children the truth about this, and it was hard to talk to them about it. All they really understood was that we lost a lot of money (they don't know how much), that it was a judgment error to make the investment, and that we learned from it. I do think that because they heard us talking about it, it probably affected them, too, in a subtle way. I'm not bitter about it, but I regret my foolishness. Over time, I've learned not to bear a grudge against some of the principals because I think it's not helpful to my family to hold onto those kinds of bad feelings. I don't even have as much interest in investing anymore mainly because there was a violation of my faith and trust. But I have learned from this and acknowledge that while it has a huge price, I can't deny the extent of the learning experience I got from it.

Like Jake, we sometimes have fantasies as investors about merging our vocation and our avocation. Some of us love our jobs and feel that our jobs are like our hobbies—that this is what we would choose to do whether we were paid or not. This is fulfilling if you are lucky enough to experience it. However, transforming your hobby into a business is a different matter entirely. To do so is to risk distracting yourself from your strengths—from your use of the knowledge and skills that constitute your expertise. That jeopardizes the process of the big master plan that we talked about earlier for using our human capital, harvesting it, and turning it into financial capital. As soon as we become derailed with a second business enterprise, our focus is no longer in the area that we previously identified as our greatest leverage.

There are exceptions. Some people are talented multitaskers who can manage multiple businesses with great focus and energy and be very successful. But you have to know if you are one of those rare people. When you take your eye off the big, established target and go after the tiny moving target, the resulting distraction could lead to extreme economic and personal costs.

As Jake mentioned, just because you like something or enjoy an activity doesn't mean you can pursue it successfully as a business. The difference between having a hobby and running a hobby as a business can be great. One of the benefits of having a hobby is that it's a stress release from the parts of your life that impose mandatory requirements. In business, you have to make a living, report to a boss, meet deadlines, and return phone calls. The beauty of a hobby is that it allows you to escape and enjoy. Whether it's sailing your boat, running in the park, or playing soccer with your kids, you can forget about everything and appreciate the experience. When that activity becomes a business, some of that carefree abandonment is lost and replaced with the more mundane aspects of any occupation. You need employees, payroll, job descriptions, and technology support. You must have specific accountability. Sometimes it's just not fun anymore.

In the financial world, when referring to potential new business opportunities, we sometimes say, "This idea looks good on paper." This means an opportunity seems like a great idea, but when you actually live it, the story is quite different. If you're clever, you'll apply your professional capabilities proficiently so that you can then buy yourself the time and the financial independence to pursue your hobby without a financial destination in mind. You can truly be free to enjoy your hobby in the way you intended and not have it conflict with your financial goals.

Jake's story may seem extreme, but similar versions happen every day. Perhaps one of the most common over the last few years involves the real estate market. An enthusiastic investor calls a friend and says, "We should buy old houses and fix them up. You have solid carpentry skills, and I'm good with people. If I could get you to do the contract work on the houses, and if I did the transactions, we could split the money we put in and we could share the profits. I think we'd make a great team. Look at all the real estate we could buy so cheaply. We'll make a ton of money. We'll rent the properties, and the values will just go up and up." You know the end of this story.

Beware the "whisper-down-the-lane" investment method. ("He's doing it, so it must be a good idea." "She's doing it, and she never makes any mistakes.") What do you really know about what other people are doing with their money? How do you know what mistakes they've made? Are they doing what they know? Are you?

Spend your time where you can grow and leverage your human capital. Be wary of situations in which your knowledge and experience are limited. Seek professional advice and be skeptical of promises about the future—especially when you are not the expert. Better yet, focus on challenges for which you already are the expert or shortly intend to become one. Do what you know and recognize what you don't know.

Chapter 6

Have Investment Rules That Work for You

In recent years, investors have been stunned by the proliferation of Ponzis and the apparent growth of financial scams. You may know the Ponzi as a slick investment scheme that pays hefty returns to some investors from money paid by subsequent investors, rather than from any actual profit earned. These events may have led you to second guess what you understood to be a trusted relationship with your advisor. You may now be questioning yourself and asking, "When I have money that is not in my immediate and direct control, what is the other person going to do with it?"

Perhaps you are wondering, "How do I avoid encountering a Ponzi scheme? How do I know I won't be involved in a Ponzi that surfaces years after I become an investor?"

One of the most obvious ways to increase your security and confidence is to establish rules for the management of your investments. These rules have to apply to your life and what makes sense to you, so you may have to make some adjustments to the six simple rules that constitute this chapter.

Still, these rules as written should work for 80% of investors. They are remarkably simple—not technical or complicated—and they are designed for your education and protection.

Rule #1: As the Investor, I Must Understand What I Own

If you do not understand an investment, regardless of how many times it is explained to you, in what kind of terminology, and by whom, do not buy it. You wait to buy it until you understand it. If you can understand it, then you should be able to assess risk, and that's the most important component of this rule. You must evaluate what could happen, positive and negative, and how you would be affected.

Sometimes the risk can be accompanied by illiquidity. For example, you might think you have a liquid asset, but maybe you did not completely understand the investment from the start. Later, you may learn that it is actually not liquid after all. In that case, your error is compounded because you misunderstood both the risk and the liquidity. When you realize that the investment is performing poorly, and you want to sell, you can't because the asset is illiquid.

It's up to the advisor to help you get to a point of understanding, but the advisor doesn't do all the work. You must also take a position of a commitment to learn. If you feel you are struggling with a concept, further discussion is necessary. The advisor can also make suggestions of ways to learn more, such as reading material, tapes, or online study. It's important to gather supportive information from an educational approach and not from anyone who's trying to sell you something.

Rule #2: I Must Understand the Degree to Which My Investments Are Truly Liquid

When your investments are liquid, you have access to the money. Liquid generally means no less than "trade plus 3 days." At any given time, you can call your advisor, make a sales transaction, and in 3 days you will have access to the funds. It's not 3 weeks, it's not "let me sign here and give you an I.O.U.," and it's not "I'll call you when the money comes in." It's "trade plus 3 days." The time frame can be even shorter. For example, cash in a money market account or a checking account generally is available immediately, without delay.

The rule that investments must be liquid won't necessarily apply to everyone. Some people invest in artwork, commodities, private equity, or real estate. But most investors require access to their investment capital and maybe also the income and growth. In fact, they may need to borrow against their investments, so they may need them to be eligible for collateral. When investments are illiquid, they may not be available to pledge against a loan. As a general rule, most investors need liquidity.

Rule #3: My Investments Should Be Completely Transparent

Transparency has risen to the forefront of investment language over the last 2 years. Recent events on Wall Street have highlighted what it means to be *not transparent*. Transparency means you can look into the inner workings of what you own and understand the small particles. For example, with a mutual fund, you can review the annual or quarterly report or get an online statement that enables you to see the individual positions within the funds. With an investment manager, you can look at the actual securities. It's not a piece of paper that says you have $100,000 in XYZ Fund and that's it. You can view the details. The reporting of the assets should come from a third-party source and not from the advisor directly. For example, most brokerage firms produce monthly or quarterly statements that flow to clients from an official and central location, bypassing the advisor. This means that the advisor cannot "touch" the data that is presented to the client. The same standards should apply to online access for account values and detail.

The point of transparency is to help you understand, through reliable data, exactly what you own. If it's not transparent, it can't be explained. If it can't be explained, you won't understand it, which reflects back on Rule #1.

Rule #4: My Investments Must Be Audited by Federal Regulators and/or an Independent Third Party

Regulation means that some official government agency has specific jurisdiction over the activity of the financial advisor and investment firm. Federal regulation should be favorable for the client's protection. Quality regulation means that someone can be held accountable for the physical safety of your assets. (This differs from market risk— what can happen to those assets based on market fluctuations.) In general, clients and advisors should welcome the components of federal regulation when it comes to securities.

Rule #5: I Must Understand How I Am Paying for Investment Advice, Services, and Products

Investments are available on all sorts of "platforms" that permit various forms of payment, depending on the advice, services, and products available. Some advisors are *transaction-based*, meaning that you pay a commission each time you purchase a product. Others are *fee-based*, meaning that you pay the advisor based on the total assets under management. In addition, some investments, such as certain mutual funds, have internal fees, sales commissions, or both. In some *separately managed accounts*, fees may be shared between the advisor and outside investment managers. In that case, the advisor acts like a traffic controller, helping the client allocate funds to individual compartments that reflect asset allocation choices. Payment choices are commonly determined by the structure of the firm where the advisor is employed, but most advisors have preferences based on philosophy, style, and personal experience.

What's the best way to understand the fees you will be paying? Ask! It's in everyone's best interest for fees to be discussed in detail at the beginning of the relationship. You want to know what advice, services, and products you are buying and for how much. That is a way to appraise the VALUE of what the advisor has to offer. The advisor, in turn, knows that a favorable pricing arrangement may contribute to the protection and growth of your capital over the long term. An advisor who is truly committed to a relationship will continually offer the highest value of advice, services, and products at a cost structure that is most beneficial to you.

If you follow Rules #1 through #5, can you still make a mistake? Of course, because there's a sixth rule, and it could be the most important one.

Rule #6: I Have Personally Investigated the Character of the People with Whom I Associate and Do Business. I Did Not Delegate This Critical Responsibility to a Third Party

In the case of Bernie Madoff's multibillion dollar Ponzi scheme that was exposed in 2008, clients knew someone who knew him, heard of him, read about him, knew someone who made a lot of money, or tried to invest with him. How many people knew him very well, associated with him intimately, spent time with him, and truly knew his character?

When you're considering an advisor, there are two basic skills sets to look for, and clients often become fixated on the one of lesser importance: the *doing* of the investments. "If I become your client, how will you invest my money? I want to see what you're going to do." This leads the advisor to recommend products, services, banking, and lending.

What is more critical than the *doing* is the way the advisor *thinks.* Anyone can follow a recipe, but only accomplished chefs are artists— culinary masters who *think* their way through complex creations. The ideal financial advisor is someone who will not merely follow an investment recipe but rather apply well-cultivated thought and intelligence to evaluate options and make masterful judgments that satisfy your investment "pallet."

Frequently, this critical component of the evaluation process is simply overlooked. When you interview an advisor (which you should be doing yourself and not delegating to someone else,) you should ask questions and dig deep.

- Tell me about your background and your business experience.
- Talk to me about the way you think.
- Explain your philosophy about investing.
- Tell me how I will pay for investments and advice.
- Tell me about your family.
- Tell me who you associate with when you're not at work.

This can be taken even further. For example, you could also interview the team or the staff of the advisor. Sit down with the team and ask them, "How does the advisor treat you? How do you like working here? How long have you been here? Why do you stay in this practice? Why do you stay with this firm?"

In addition to that, you could interview the branch manager. "How would you describe your relationship with this advisor? Why should I choose this advisor over other advisors I could consider?" The branch manager may offer an additional point of view and might have a perspective on how your needs may fit with that particular advisor.

Finally, you can speak with accountants, attorneys, or even other clients who know the advisor well. The advisor may even provide you with references. Speak with three to five individuals who have a professional history with this advisor. (Verify that they do not have a conflict of interest or a monetary connection.) You want the most independent assessments you can find. Remember, investment performance is only one aspect of an advisor's style, experience, and character.

Jason provides a perfect example of what can happen when you don't apply these rules. Jason is a 55-year-old businessman who benefited from the sale of his family's business, where he also worked for many years. He invested the money with several institutions, and the investments seemed to produce above average returns for a while. When the economy weakened, and his investments faltered, Jason went to a new advisor with his portfolio to assess the standing of his investments and get advice. He was concerned because the value of his accounts had deteriorated rapidly, and as a result, he was reconsidering his relationships with his former advisors.

Looking at his portfolio, the advisor recognized that Jason had invested most of his money in investments that were neither liquid nor transparent. It was clear that Jason didn't understand what he owned. The investments had not been audited, Jason had no idea what he was paying, and he had not personally investigated the character of the advisory professionals.

When someone shows me a portfolio full of investments that violate these basic principles, it's like looking at a once-beautiful field that's never been properly maintained and is full of weeds and rocks. It's difficult to face because I know what it could have been and what it is now. I also know what it's going to take to fix it. To repair a field that has been mismanaged for 50 years, you would have to dig the entire thing up. And after you do, there may be only one pile of useable topsoil, and the rest is just waste.

Jason didn't even realize that his investments were not transparent. He didn't know they were illiquid and going to be worth half of the value he estimated. Jason's portfolio included a variety of high-risk investments, including millions that had gone to a feeder fund and then to Bernard Madoff. If he had followed these rules, he would never have had these investments in the first place.

You can hear Jason's dismay as he shares his assessment of the events.

Jason: I realize now that I should have paid much more attention. I was so focused on making money that I neglected to follow the simplest rules. Ironically, when I was in business, I knew exactly how to develop rules and follow them. That's why my business was so successful and I was able to sell it so profitably! I now understand that I have to remake myself financially and be more of an active advocate for my interests. You can be sure that I will have rules and stick to them for the rest of my investing days!

Another investor, Martin, a conservative and experienced entrepreneur, summarizes this point especially well.

Martin: It only takes the experience of losing money to learn the value of having rules. I learned this early, the hard way. Through my values, life experience, and examples I've set,

I've passed this on to my children so that they can avoid making the same mistakes.

You have to have rules to have a basis for selecting the right investments and the most suitable advisory professionals. Develop rules for yourself, establish a discipline, and monitor your course. You'll find this to be one of the most valuable ways to protect your investments, for yourself, and your family.

Chapter 7

The Time to Have the Fire Drill Is Not in the Middle of the Fire

We've talked about the need for prioritization, planning, and responsibility. How do we manage these, considering our emotional reactions to the changing investment world? The answer is that we must do the most difficult planning first, when we can think clearly and have opportunities to evaluate our strategy. Then, the consequences are small. When there is no pressure or need for immediate reaction, we can contemplate various options and discuss them with family members and advisors. Unfortunately we don't always use this time effectively because we are preoccupied with other pressing tasks—or because we somehow just don't get around to taking action regarding what we claim to value. Then suddenly a matter transforms from a long-term issue to an urgent need, and we might find ourselves unprepared. This applies across many levels of investing and includes subjects such as communication with advisors; wills and estate planning; tax planning; protection of spouses and gifting to children and charitable interests; and asset allocation and investment strategy.

These issues are the most important to consider early on because they can become the most problematic if you don't deal with them when they seem far in the future. It's an ironic predicament because when an issue is far in the future it looks small and loses your attention to some other current, demanding matter that has your focus. But as the future comes closer, this tiny snowball gathers more snow around it. Suddenly you're standing at the base of the hill, and a giant snowball is rolling right toward your head! And you're thinking, "Why didn't I deal with this when it was an ice chip?" Now that it's become an emergency, you're not in the right frame of mind to cope. Your thinking is compromised, and you may feel overwhelmed.

It's quite easy to get into a cycle where small issues get out of control. Have you ever heard someone say, "I don't have time to plan; I'm too busy putting out fires?" That's essentially what happens. When you are faced with urgent considerations, other items that still need your attention are not in the queue. Eventually, they expand, and they're burning right in front of you while another small issue is developing. You get in a vicious firefighting cycle, and eventually all you can do is just stand there and aim the hose!

Some of this panic can be avoided if you have contingency plans already in place. But how can you get to a contingency plan if you haven't completed the basic plan? In other words, how can you execute the fire escape plan if you've never done the drill? Let's look at these issues one by one and talk about how to practice a more effective approach.

Communication with Advisors

Think back to our earlier discussion about transparency. This concept also applies to the way you communicate with your advisors. This means setting expectations in the beginning of the relationship about how you're going to communicate, what the frequency will be, and what you expect to get out of each one of those communications. What communication will occur in writing? What's going to happen verbally? When is email an acceptable way to correspond? Sometimes you may find yourself harboring feelings that you're either afraid to express or can't find the words for. This can apply to both investors and advisors. Sometimes we walk around festering with feelings of frustration, anger, disappointment, or even just confusion, and we don't know how to articulate our feelings to others. If we continue for a long time like this, our line of communication deteriorates. When we have a new problem or a serious issue that requires us to communicate effectively, we can't because we failed to nurture constructive dialogue when conditions were ideal.

In the investment world, we have a popular expression, "Your first loss is your least loss." This means it is critical to deal immediately with problems before they have a chance to escalate. Each time we have a little break in the communication chain, we have to view it as an opportunity to promptly improve our interaction process and strengthen the relationship. We are preparing for times when we'll need our communication to be on super autopilot. In an emergency situation, we need all our resources focused on solving problems and on a clear common language we can rely on.

Sarah explains her experience with this.

Sarah: I had been running my own printing and graphics business for many years, and I am the first to admit that I've had little interest in investing. Most of my capital went into my business, so my liquid assets were not significant. Still, I was in the communications business, and I know how important this issue is! I felt that I had to find the right person to guide me, and it took quite a search to identify an advisor who spoke my language and used simple terms I could understand. Then, suddenly, I was faced with the death of both my parents at the same time and a complex estate and substantial inheritance. I was an only child, with no other family support, and I had to cope with this great loss and new found financial responsibility. My parents had always given me the impression that their assets were modest, and I was unprepared for the job of managing such a large sum. Luckily, I had established a relationship with a trusted advisor before this happened.

I can't imagine how I would have been able to interview people, study performance, and evaluate communication styles while all this crazy and painful stuff was happening. I was so grateful I had taken the time to do this when there were no distractions. I never thought I would need advice as much as I actually did.

Wills and Estate Planning

This is the kind of planning that you may view as a late life need that does not apply until well into the future. This wishful thinking keeps you from having to face difficult and sensitive decisions. It almost always brings up complicated family issues, and the easiest thing to do is just put it off. But what happens when someone is suffering from an illness or dies unexpectedly? What about a divorce or a family issue involving wealth disposition among heirs? When the wills and the estate planning process are not up to date, and a critical event occurs, it is almost impossible to go back after the fact and "fix" what should have been done previously.

This happened to Thomas, an investor who had been passionately committed to land conservation in his community for many years. He intended to leave a large land parcel to a local nonprofit organization dedicated to protecting open space. He talked about it frequently: "I'm going to leave this, and I'm going to do that," but he never got around to doing it. On his death, the property went to his heirs, who promptly sold it and divided it as they did the other monetary assets. That real estate is now a housing development. Thomas never completed the documentation that would have permanently preserved that real estate. The sad fact is that preservation of open space was one of Thomas' greatest passions. He lost an opportunity for a special legacy because the necessary planning never made it to the top of his list.

Tax Planning

Tax planning is another issue that can get pushed back behind other priorities. Superior tax planning requires being in strong communication with your advisor and your accountant about your investment income and capital gains picture. Your accountant may need information from your advisor to accurately prepare the schedule of estimated tax payments. When your accountant and financial advisor work together, your needs can be addressed in a proactive way that keeps you current and prepared for what you owe or can save in taxes. No one wants to write an unexpected big check due to poor planning, especially if the money hasn't been set aside! This is avoidable by planning up front (1) how you're going to handle your taxes, (2) who's going to account for the figures, (3) how it's going to be communicated, and (4) how it's going to be paid for.

Protection of Spouses and Gifting to Children and Charitable Interests

Protecting spouses and gifting to children and charities involves another complex series of decisions that require thought and examination. On one hand, we've worked hard for our assets, and perhaps our first thought is that we want to see them transferred to our heirs in their entirety. On the other hand, we recognize that we're facing estate taxes and sometimes even taxes for current gifts. We want to make sure our spouses have the protection of a sufficient asset base for liabilities, lifestyle needs, and the support of the children. When the children are older, we don't want to provide a disincentive for them to perform economically by inundating them with too much money before they have the maturity to manage it. This is a delicate discussion that needs to take place between you, your financial advisor, your accountant, and your legal counsel. There are many strategies that can help to transfer assets from your name to your heirs without giving them the assets right now, but these are techniques that need to be contemplated when you are alive, of sound mind, and in a financial position to make these transitions. These kinds of decisions should not be put off for too long, particularly if they also involve life insurance. As you age, you run the risk of becoming ill and possibly uninsurable, and then it's too late.

Asset Allocation and Investment Strategy

Asset allocation is the strategy used to divide investments among four generally accepted classes: cash, bonds, stocks, and hard assets such as real estate or collectibles. Each class has its own distinguishing characteristics, risks, and historical rates of return. There can also be variance within each class. For example, small cap stocks may outperform large cap stocks. Cash, bonds, and stocks are usually considered to be "liquid," and hard assets "illiquid." The benefits of each class must be considered along with the commensurate risks and costs. Interestingly, these asset classes often work in complementary styles so that while one or two are not performing well, others may be. Occasionally they all seem to work well together, as they did in 1995. And sometimes, nothing seems to work at all, as in the second half of 2008!

Let's review the features and risks of each asset class. With cash, you generally have liquidity and safety. However, you may receive very low returns because you've made no investment "commitment." In addition, you are accepting other risks, such as the effects of inflation, (we'll talk more about that later), and opportunity cost. Opportunity cost is the price paid for NOT capitalizing on other investment opportunities. Over the last 100 years, cash has averaged about 3% annually.

Bonds are instruments of credit: When you buy bonds you are lending money to another party, such as the government, a municipality, or a corporation. The quality of that entity may define its "creditworthiness," or likelihood of your being repaid. In exchange for the loan you've made, you receive interest—and on some predetermined date in the future, you expect the return of your principal. Bonds are disinflationary because the principal is likely to be repaid with dollars that have less purchasing power as a result of inflation. Also, if interest rates are rising, the market value of your bonds may fall as new bonds are offered at higher available rates. On the other hand, bonds are often desired for their safety, income, and predictability, as illustrated by their 5% annual rate of return over the last 100 years.

Stocks are a residual asset: When you buy stocks you are investing in a company by buying a fraction of it. Ideally, you seek companies with earnings growth and subsequent price appreciation. Some stocks pay dividends, and this can contribute handsomely to the overall rate of return, which has averaged about 9.5% over the last 100 years. Stocks are considered to be long-term investments. When you buy stocks, you give up some of the predictability of cash and bonds to increase the potential of long-term returns. Stocks do well in environments of inflation, and they can be quite liquid. However, even the best-run companies' stock prices can be significantly affected by the economy, the changes in industry, and the whims of the financial markets. That is why you sometimes hear investors refer to the stock market with gambling jargon, such as "playing the market," "losing one's shirt," and so on. They refer to the investor's lack of control over price volatility and frustration when these investments disappoint. However, among the liquid asset classes, stocks are historically the best performing asset over long periods of time.

Hard assets, such as real estate and collectibles, also have the potential to yield high rates of return. These assets generally require specialized expertise and can be complicated by illiquidity and tax considerations. Although they are not the focus of this book, they deserve a place in your overall planning and investment strategy.

Now, let's mix and match some of the liquid assets to see what happens. What returns might you expect over long periods of time if 30% of your assets were in bonds and 70% were in stocks? Try this:

Multiply 30% by 5% (bonds) and add it to 70% by 9.5% (stocks). What do you get? 8.15%, a return you might expect with that asset allocation.

Now try this one:

Multiply 80% by 5% (bonds) and add it to 20% by 9.5% (stocks). What's the answer? 5.9%.

How about this one:

Multiply 80% by 3% (cash) and add it to 20% by 5% (bonds). 3.4%!

It's obvious that these combinations have dramatically different historical rates of return, accompanied by varying risk levels. This is what advisors mean when they say that asset allocation is one of the most influential factors in portfolio performance.

Your asset allocation and investment strategy are perhaps the most obvious illustrations of the importance of advance planning, and they can also be the most challenging. This is because these decisions have to be made and then continually reevaluated. If you think that you can establish a strategy and then be "done" with it, you will surely be disappointed! Asset allocation and investment strategy require consistent review and long-term planning. The "drills" continue throughout your entire investment life! Let's look at an example of how this works.

Shelly and Bob start out with $1 million. Their goal is to have $2 million in 11 years. This is so that they can live on an income stream of about $90,000 per year in their retirement, or 4.5% of their capital. That means they need a 6.5% return on investments over the next 11 years to accumulate two million from the starting balance of one million.

Based on history, the probability of obtaining this return is highest with an asset allocation of at least 50% stocks, and 50% (or nearly so) in fixed income. So they move ahead with this investment strategy, which is sensible given their assets and goals. Because they have children in college and limited resources, they cannot save much during this period. This means that they will be very dependent on the actual investment returns. If they happen to be investing during a positive market environment, they might earn a return even higher than 6.5%. From 2003 to 2007 the stock market appreciated over 80%. If their stock investments do perform this way, their asset allocation will change. That's because the 50% that is in stocks will dramatically outperform the fixed income investments. So within 3 or 4 years, if there is no change to the allocations, they won't be 50/50 anymore. They'll be 60/40, or even 65/35. Somewhere along the line, a decision needs to be made about rebalancing. But ironically, this peak arrives at a time when it is most difficult for investors to make these changes. Why? Because they're making so much money! If they reduce those securities that have appreciated, they are also going to pay capital gains taxes. Here is where emotions can get the best of them. This moment when there is the most exuberance, the most money, and the least balance is exactly the time the over-weighted asset class (in this case, equities) should be sold to bring the portfolio back into line. This process can be challenging, and investors may need a reminder that the long-term goals must be firmly in focus.

There's no hard and fast rule as to how frequently a portfolio needs to be rebalanced. This has to be worked out with the client and the advisor, and it's often influenced by the investor's time frame, tax picture, risk tolerance, and stage of life. But in general, portfolios get rebalanced at least annually to coordinate with tax obligations.

What if Shelly and Bob start with a 50/50 allocation and the market has some very negative years? If they find themselves with only 35% in equities, what do you think they should do? If they are not yet at retirement and have the appropriate risk tolerance, they should buy stocks because now they're over-weighted in bonds. (If they are at a late stage, they are forced by their lack of planning to wait for recovery and make adjustments later when the cycle may have reversed.) It's likely that the bonds will have outperformed the equities, so they'll probably have capital gains in those bonds. They need to sell bonds and buy stocks. They are doing that when equities are historically low and underperforming. This is often when public opinion is going the opposite way—in other words, at what feels like the worst time. We've seen over the years that the right investment decisions almost always feel completely wrong at the time we are making them!

Now, imagine another scenario. What if their investments appreciate significantly and Shelly and Bob don't rebalance? They start out at a 50/50 allocation. The strong stock market takes them to 65%, and they decide to "ride the crest of the wave." Now the 65% stock position increases their risk, and as the market corrects, they lose substantial capital and miss the chance to "harvest" their gains.

There's your fire. And there's been no drill. There's not much that an advisor can do for you when an over-weighted position compromises the integrity of the strategy, and the bubble bursts.

This can apply to real estate, art, or any other assets. This is what advisors mean when they talk about diversification and about not relying on any single asset class—even cash—to achieve your investment goals. It's critical that you recognize that assets come in and out of favor and can work in complementary and also oppositional styles. By viewing the entire portfolio periodically and making adjustments that put you back in balance, you're essentially performing fire drills on your investments instead of waiting until your portfolio is on fire to make a change.

Making adjustments is difficult and challenging because of the emotional component of the investing process. Remember, you won't have to get out of trouble if you have the forethought to avoid trouble in the first place! It is an advisor's role to help you manage your emotions, so you can look at the facts and maintain a more objective approach, but you are ultimately in charge of your plans and your destiny!

Chapter 8

The Best Advice Is Sometimes About What Not to Do

In August 2000, Edward contacted an advisor he had researched, with a desire to transfer his investments. The advisor evaluated his investments, helped him organize his goals, and designed an investment strategy that allocated about 60% of his money to the stock market and 40% to fixed income. Right about that time, the market began to deteriorate, and stocks performed very poorly over the next 2½ years. Edward handled this well, but it had to be tough on him, and of course the advisor was frustrated, particularly because the relationship was new. As the markets became more and more difficult, the advisor became even more discouraged and began to second guess the strategy.

Shortly after the September 11 terrorist attacks on the United States, one of the most difficult periods for all investors and advisors—for all Americans—Edward called the advisor and started the conversation by saying, "I'm calling to thank you."

"Thank me!" the advisor exclaimed. "What could you possibly be talking about? I feel so terrible about what's happened over the last year, and I'm doing my best to navigate it, but I'm very disappointed."

Edward said, "No, you don't understand. You forgot about some other advice you gave me. You told me not to invest $600,000, the minimum required in a private equity partnership that I was seriously considering. I've just learned that the investment has been a total failure. My friends who invested $600,000 have lost all their capital. You strongly discouraged me from considering this investment. You told me that it was outside of my risk parameters and that the illiquidity could be problematic. Even though my stock market investments are down, I know that I own shares in high-quality companies, so these assets are likely to recover. This other investment will never regain its value. Of all the advice you have given me, this guidance of what **not** to do has been the greatest value."

Sometimes when you look at what you expect from an advisor, the understanding is that you will be getting recommendations to buy this, buy that, do this, or do that. But there's more to investing than what you do. There's also what you should *not* do.

We've already discussed that investments should be maintained in an overall strategy that includes rules. The rules should say not only which investments are *in*, but also which investments are *out*. There should be reasoning for this, generally having to do with risk evaluation and timeframe. The key always comes back to what is in your strategy and what is not. If an investment does not deserve inclusion into your strategy, there is a reason for that. To justify including that investment in your strategy, you need to either make an exception to your rules or change your rules. Otherwise you're violating your rules. Part of an advisor's job is not just to tell you what to do but to make sure you don't take an action that will violate your rules.

Right now you might be thinking, "Wait a minute. After all, this is my money. What if I get a hunch or an idea I want to act on? As the client, aren't I in charge?" We know investing, to a great degree, is driven by emotions. Sometimes the timing may not be ideal, or you may want to put too much money into your hunch or idea. Sometimes you want to act on a lot of hunches or ideas. We advisors help you manage and balance your instincts with what we believe to be best for you in the long run. We don't want to get into a battle with you about who's in charge. That question has already been decided. You are in charge. Your advisor serves you. But we are here to offer advice that protects you, and sometimes that might mean protecting you from yourself.

What are some examples of circumstances in which you might need that kind of protection? Here are a few to consider.

Investing with Friends

I sometimes hear investors say, "I've invested with friends before. We've always gotten along. We've made a pact never to let anything come between us in our relationship." Have you ever heard this? My experience has shown repeatedly that when an investment goes south, the friendship goes with it.

This friends-and-business issue is parallel to the hobbies-and-business issue illustrated in Chapter 5, "Do What You Know and Recognize What You Don't Know," with Jake's boat-building venture. Although hobby-like enjoyment of one's business is healthy, Jake found that trying to parlay a hobby into a business may not be. Similarly, although friendships developed within a business can breed camaraderie, expanding a friendship into a business partnership carries great risks. You might remember that Jake lost on both counts: After the failed venture, he lost interest in boating and in the marina and finally even in the friends with whom he collaborated.

Do not invest with friends. Avoid investment clubs with friends. If possible, do not be in a business with your friends. If you are in a business relationship with someone who along the way happens to become your friend, that has merit, but in your discussions, conversations, meetings, and activities, remember to identify which hat you are wearing—the business partner hat or the friendship hat. It takes a lot of experience, professionalism, and maturity to take one hat off and put the other one on consistently while remembering which hat you are wearing.

You are better off not putting yourself in that situation in the first place. Instead, maintain your professional relationships separate from friendships. Let friendships develop from these professional relationships and then get practice being a friend with someone who already has a professional relationship with you. That is a good way to test your skills in wearing both hats. Don't start out by trying to transform a friendship into a business relationship. That can end painfully—and with lasting effects.

Overextending Your Borrowing

Another danger to avoid is over-leverage. This means continuing to make new purchases by using various forms of credit, ranging from mortgages to securities loans to credit cards. It can become an escalating habit after you get a taste for acquiring more and more with money you don't actually have.

Borrowing has its advantages because it permits you to benefit from leverage. This means you can be in two (or more!) places at once by owning more than what you could without the extension of credit. You can have the house and the car. You can buy a building and invest in a business. But then you have to manage the expenses and risks commensurate with those commitments. That amounts to a variety of factors that sometimes act in opposition and create new stresses outside those you bargained for! The variables include, but are not limited to

- Cost of the debt (interest rate)
- Terms (fixed, variable, time frame, fees to borrow)
- Value/carrying costs of the asset(s) you used to acquire the debt
- Value/carrying costs of the assets(s) collateralizing the debt

In addition, you have the future burden of determining how and when you will repay the debt. Will you do that from your savings, your salary, or the income from one or more of the assets? You may plan to sell one of the assets to offset your obligation.

The combination of unexpected expenses and errors in managing cash flow contributed to Dennis and Arlene's predicament. Dennis, 60, and Arlene, 55, purchased their ultimate retirement home with a variable rate mortgage at a low interest rate. With the debt service so modest, they could afford a more expensive home, and this meant they had an even smaller down payment. When the home appreciated, they obtained a home equity loan and used the increased equity to add a screened-in porch for entertaining. Just as adjustable mortgage interest rates started to rise, Dennis' company was acquired by a conglomerate, and he was laid off from his job of 30 years. In adjusting to the rising monthly payments, Dennis and Arlene used their credit cards to cover expenses, but the credit card rates were even higher. And as you might have guessed, the value of their home went down, so there was no equity available to refinance and reorganize their debt. Where has this left them?

> **Dennis:** I keep thinking that this is just a bad dream, and any minute I am going to wake up. We've been seriously contemplating bankruptcy. Our house is worth $450,000, down from our purchase price of $565,000. Our mortgage, home equity, and credit card debt total over $435,000. My severance pay lasted only 6 months, and that's long gone. I've had to invade my IRA, which of course means I'm paying added taxes, but I feel I have no choice. I have to do to something about these credit card payments. I can't believe how unlucky we were; the housing market fell apart just as adjustable mortgage interest rates went up, and then I lost my job. Even if I wanted to sell the house to get rid of the debt, who's buying houses now? We're stuck.

You may be thinking, "How could they get themselves into such a ridiculous situation?" But the fact is, many Americans have faced, are facing, and will face issues just like those of Dennis and Arlene. How can you avoid this? Let's review some strategies that can help you make safer debt management choices.

- Leave yourself a healthy margin of equity against what you plan to borrow. See if you can live with reducing your indebtedness by 15% to 20% of your original intention as a protective buffer.

- Evaluate carefully ALL the moving parts. The debt service is only one consideration. Other variables, such as the costs to carry assets and changing market values, can significantly affect your financial condition. When market conditions become unfavorable, selling investments to cover the debt can be difficult because the assets may become less liquid and also decrease in value.

- Envision "worst-case scenarios" before accepting new debt obligations. Think of everything that could go wrong and brainstorm how you would cope. Be realistic! If you can't handle it in your imagination, what makes you think reality will be easier?

- Have an "end game" regarding your debt. When and how are you paying this back? Make a plan and stick to it. You may even have to tell yourself, "no new debts until I pay off the ones I have." Impose personal limits on yourself, separate and distinct from those required by lending institutions.

- Finally, think carefully about protecting your long-term security before taking on any new responsibilities.

Living the Consequences of Someone Else's Choices

All choices, including investments, have consequences. While you're managing the consequences of your own actions, you need to be careful not to inadvertently sign up for more consequences than you planned. This is sometimes illustrated in cases of parents who want to be supportive of their young adult children. In a slow economy, young adults may find their entrée into the workforce disappointing. They may have aspired to an exciting career and now are waiting tables. They may have loans and obligations, yet want to continue with the lifestyle they had when they were dependents. No parents want their children to struggle, so it's tempting to be drawn into assisting financially while they are "getting on their feet." But that frequently expands to taking on new expenses, such as educational costs for advanced degrees, cars and car insurance, apartments, travel, bills—and before you know it, cumulative sums that in some cases exceed the parents' lifestyle costs! This poses two problems: (1) the parents end up "living" the consequences of their children's' choices, creating personal and financial stress, and (2) the children avoid "living" the consequences of their own choices, losing the opportunity to learn and grow from the experience. Although it's critical for each of us to "own" our consequences, we should not take on what is not ours in the interest of making things easier for those we care about. We have to make the distinction between "a little temporary help in a pinch" and an open-ended relationship of dependence. Finding that line will make life better for everyone in the long run.

Getting Attached to Things and Not Wanting to Sell

Sometimes investors hesitate to sell investments for sentimental or personal reasons, even when the financial reasons and original logic for holding these investments no longer apply.

Adam and Louise were very attached to their house in the northeastern mountains, and they wanted to keep it, even though the house was costing them $70,000 a year to maintain, and they weren't using it in the way they had when their children were younger. They thought, "We want to keep it for the kids!" But the kids weren't using it either. One lived in California, one in New York City, and one in New Mexico. How much sense did it make to keep a house worth $1.3 million in the hopes that one or more of the kids would move back home? Were they thinking that the house was an incentive for the kids to move closer? The mountain home had been a special family gathering place with many wonderful memories. They had to work through whether it made sense for them to continue owning this house. After 30 years, it was very, very difficult for them to sell it. But they finally admitted, "Although this is such a difficult emotional decision, it is probably the best move for us."

Adam and Louise put the house on the market and sold it in 2006. Shortly thereafter, the market in the mountains changed dramatically, as real estate prices declined for the first time in many years. The house they sold for $1.3 million wouldn't go for $750,000 in the 2008 market. Meanwhile, Adam's health unexpectedly deteriorated, and he was diagnosed with degenerative disc disease. This limited his ability to do surgery or practice medicine, and he had to leave his career and go on disability.

What if Adam and Louise still had that vacation home, with new health-care expenses, and Adam unable to work? They are so lucky to have sold that house when the market was at a high point! They were smart to honestly examine whether that house made them truly happy and whether it was worth the financial risk.

Adam and Louise's investment decision ended well, but it's important to realize that they escaped disaster by taking the advice about what *not* to do. With guidance and support from their advisor, they detached themselves from a possession that no longer held the same value. As a result of this experience, they reconsidered all their attachments and priorities, particularly in light of Adam's health condition. This led them to focus their time, money, and energy on their most important goals.

There's risk in both giving and receiving the advice about what not to do. It takes discipline and strength to say no to an opportunity. You have to have a strong footing and solid confidence in your investment strategy and the security of the relationship with the advisor, who may be urging you to hold back and say no.

What about when your instincts (or advisor) tell you not to do something, and it turns out that doing it would have been a good decision after all? What if a "yes" turns out to have been better financially than the "no?" Going back to one of our earlier chapters, remember the example of a child who runs between two parked cars. The point of the advice isn't about whether this one opportunity or that single investment turns out well. The point of the strategy is that you would have to take risk to engage in that activity. Advisors who tell you to avoid an action are most likely assessing the risk and giving you a calculation of the probability of success or failure. It's possible that the risk is high, the advisor says no, you proceed anyway, and the result turns out to be favorable. But over long periods of time, if the advisor is accurate in that risk calculation and in knowing you, the client, most of the advice is going to be right.

Robert is a self-employed businessman who credits his advisor with the ability to coach him on what not to do and to hold him to his investment strategy. He tells the story of how his advisor reacted to the sudden turn in the 2008 market and how he responded.

Robert: About 6 months ago, my advisor called, saying, "I feel really bad about everything that's gone on over this past year. Even though only 45% of your money is in equities, I feel terrible about what's happened. I wish there had been some way to better assess the magnitude of what was coming."

I told my advisor, "Yes, it's true that this was a much more serious correction than what you were expecting. But professionals everywhere agree that they weren't prepared for the meltdown. When I look back at our 15-year relationship, and the advice you've given me, including what you've told me to do, as well as not to do, your overall track record is impressive. What I'll remember most is all the times you've protected me and kept me from doing something that could have derailed our entire investment strategy. That's far more important to me than missing one short-term swing, even a very dramatic one."

As you can see from the preceding discussion, little pieces of advice over many years can add up to a much more substantial financial result. A financial advisor can be a valuable partner for an investor, particularly when it comes to managing the psychological twists and turns of investing with respect to long-term goals. But even if you don't have a formal financial advisor, the same message applies. You can simulate the experience by using someone else to play the same role. It might be a mentor, a confidant, or an objective family member—or even yourself, if you are strong willed. Find someone who can be your Jiminy Cricket.

If you'll remember from the story *Pinocchio*, Jiminy Cricket plays the role of conscience. If you don't have a second-party Jiminy available to you, you can even put yourself in that role by separating out your emotions and taking an analytical approach. Take some time outside of the heat of the moment when you can put aside your emotions and consider the decision objectively. Sit quietly with a pad and a pen and ask yourself, "What is my gut telling me?" Do the old exercise of drawing a line down the center of the page and writing the advantages on the left side and the disadvantages on the right side. What does this analysis reveal? Ask yourself, "Have I thought this through completely?" After you've done that, get another perspective. Show your list to a trusted friend and ask, "Do you think I'm missing anything? Tell me all the things that can go wrong." Or ask, "Who do you think I can talk with to get an idea of the potential risks of this idea I'm contemplating?"

In life, we seek relationships with people who will support what we want and maybe even help us to get it. The most valuable advice comes from those who support your intentions while watching your back. This kind of person, rather than being concerned with pleasing you or telling you what you want to hear, will tell you when an idea may not be in your best interests. Your financial advisor should fit into this role by advising you on both what to do and what not to do.

Chapter 9

Appreciate the Value of Holding on to What You Have

What's the most important rule about investing? *Don't lose the money.* When you think about everything that went into your ability to save and invest, you realize that the money represents respect for what you have accomplished as an investor. We've already talked a little about the transition from human capital to financial capital, and we're all aware that as you get older the opportunities for replacing money you've lost may be diminished.

What are all the ways you could lose money?

You Could Misplace It

How many people lose $20 bills because they put them in a pair of pants and forget about them? They go into a pocket 5 years later and say, "Look at this! I have a $20 bill in here!" Has that ever happened to you? It's not that hard to lose money. In June 2009, you may have heard the story of the "million-dollar mattress." An Israeli woman, Annat, bought a new mattress as a surprise gift for her elderly mother. When it was delivered, Annat had the tattered, old mattress hauled away as garbage. The gesture ended up bankrupting her mother, who kept nearly $1 million in the bed for decades. A relentless search of the two major dump sites in Tel Aviv was fruitless. Perhaps the mattress has been found by another ambitious person hunting through 2,500 tons of garbage per day.

You Could Waste It

Think of all the things we buy that we don't need, such as clothes we buy, and say, "I'll wear it when…" (and we don't). The trendy things we get seduced into acquiring…the food we order that we couldn't possibly eat…things we purchase and never get around to returning even if they're the wrong size, the wrong type, or they don't work right…investments we make without proper consideration and planning. Waste is so well integrated into our culture that we've lost track of its frequency and magnitude.

You Could Lose It in the Financial Markets

We have all made poor investments at one time or another; anyone can do this. You can lose money by simply not doing research and not having goals. You can be in the wrong place at the wrong time, with a lack of patience. You could underestimate the liquidity, volatility, and risk of your investment choices.

You Could Have It Stolen from You

Some investors have had money stolen by people who were ostensibly watching it for them. That goes back to the rules we've discussed so far about choosing the right advisors and associates. Who has your money? Do you really know them?

You Could Gamble It Away

Gambling is a risk you may decide to take. Gambling can be as simple as going outside on an overcast day without an umbrella. When you gamble, either the chances for winning should be very, very high, or the consequences for losing should be very, very low. If you go out without an umbrella on a cloudy day, you might get rained on, but it's not going to kill you. If you continue driving through an intersection as the light is turning from yellow to red, that could really hurt you— and also someone else. That's a foolish gamble. So is buying stocks with money that you know you'll need soon for a set expense such as taxes or a down payment on a home.

You Could Give It Away

Make sure when you give money away you give it freely—because you want to. Giving it is different than lending it, which is yet another way to lose money.

You Could Lend It and Not Get Repaid

Sometimes we don't want to face ourselves and admit that we made a loan to the wrong party. We call it a gift, and then we can absolve ourselves of poor judgment. But was it really a gift, or did we make a poor choice about the person to whom we made the loan? If you decide to reject Shakespeare's advice, "Neither a borrower nor a lender be," at least be a careful lender who discriminates perceptively among potential borrowers.

Holding on While Getting Ahead

Investors sometimes get focused on only one side of the equation: making money. They can lose sight of what's far more important: not losing it. Focusing on keeping the money is like an emergency brake on your emotions. If you pulled this brake more often, would you be less inclined to make errors? Knowing what you have as a goal can also slow down your spending, especially if it's impulsive or extravagant. If you can hold onto what you have, you can keep moving forward. If you lose it, you're relegated to "getting back to where you were," and this means climbing out of a hole. Sometimes you can never get back. For example, in 2008 the key to successful investing was to lose as little as possible. Those investors who did lose less may participate more substantially in the turnaround as it occurs. They can potentially recover at a much faster rate.

Let's take a look at how losing can affect you in dollars. (Sometimes we get distracted by percentages, and we forget to do the actual math.) Andy has $100,000 to invest. He's young. He doesn't need investment income, and he wants to be aggressive. He invests $100,000 in the international equity market. (Put aside for the moment whether you think this is a sensible strategy.) If he made this investment in early 2008, by the end of 2008 his $100,000 was worth about $55,000. This means he lost 45% of the value, or $45,000. If this investment rebounds by 45%, he doesn't get back to $100,000. It's 45% of $55,000. So that only takes him back to just shy of $80,000. Do you see how working in percentages can be deceptive? If you lost 45% last year, and you gained 45% this year, you don't have your original investment back!

When you develop a portfolio strategy with an advisor, you place your investment trust in that person. It's as if you were handing delicate little birds to the advisor to hold, and saying, "I'll be back later for the birds. When I come back I want to see healthier, bigger, better birds who know how to fly, but don't give me anything less than I've given you to watch over." When you come back for the birds later, at the very least you want to know the birds are still there!

But here's something else we may forget to consider. What condition are *we* in? What has changed in your life between the time you dropped off the birds and the time you come back to get them?

Things can change in your life, and you could need something that you don't need right now. Or you might be unable to fulfill your responsibilities in the way that you can now. The birds are only one component of a much larger picture.

The best balance is to focus on both sides of the equation—holding onto what you have while making it grow. Investing is not a substitute for working. It is harvesting the product of your work.

Another example of one-sided investment thinking can be illustrated with the Rule of 72. If you divide 72 by your interest rate, the answer is how many years it will take your money to double. For example, 7.2% (an estimated interest rate) divided into 72 gives you a doubling in 10 years. (The inverse is also true. You can put the number of years into 72, and it tells you what your interest rate would have to be.)

The Rule of 72

72 ÷ Interest Rate = Years to Double

or

72 ÷ Years to Double = Interest Rate

For example, let's say that one of your goals is to double your money every 6 years with a plan to retire in 18 years. If you doubled your money every 6 years, you could double it three times in this next 18 years. So take the number 72, and divide it by 6. We get the interest rate of 12%. That means you have to make 12% for 18 years because you're going to get 12% for the first 6 years, then 12% for the next 6, and 12% for the third 6. Is that a realistic assumption? Probably not. The stock market over 100 years has produced a 9.5% rate of return, and the bond market about 5%. If half of your money is in equities and half of your money is in bonds, a more reasonable expectation is 7.25%, which means your money is likely to double about every 10 years. So if you have an 18-year time frame, you're going to get a little less than two doubles, not three.

Sometimes investors get so focused on this doubling and the ultimate financial goal that they fail to take into consideration what can happen if they lose what they have and how that can erode the outcome as compared to their expectations. How do you align your expectations with reality? Expand your time frame, save more money, or start sooner, but don't opt for an unrealistic expectation. It's the unrealistic expectation that leads you to get further and further away from the most important point, which is not losing your money in the first place.

Listen to investors Arthur and Rachel. Arthur is an advisor to real estate partnerships, and his education includes an MBA (masters of business administration) and a CPA (certified public accountant). He has a high intellect and extensive experience with complex financial transactions. Rachel is an executive in the medical wholesale supply industry. With more than 20 years of investment experience, they've thought of themselves as progressive and sophisticated.

Arthur: I've been working from home for many years, using state-of-the-art technology in my business. Information about my investments was easily accessible. I have always been a dedicated student of the financial markets, and I actively read and follow the media regarding investments. I got involved in making my own investment decisions without the help of an advisor. Over the years, I developed an aggressive strategy for investing in options. I had some success with this during the 1990s and gained confidence in my trading skills during this upswing. At the same time, I was spending much of my day trading, instead of consulting, which is what I do best. During this time I developed a false reality by thinking that my skills in business could be instinctively transferred into the investment field. Success in one arena does not automatically breed success in another.

Suddenly, when the market environment changed, I found myself unable to react fast enough to what was happening. I felt like a very good swimmer who was quickly in water that was way too deep. Looking back, I recognize I never actually considered the possibility that I could lose basically everything in this very aggressive strategy. The psychological toll of this was devastating, and it was a serious distraction to my professional obligations.

Rachel: I was really annoyed with him. I can't believe how far he let this thing get. I blamed him, and I was worried we were going to be wiped out because we had already lost half of our investment value. This was so much more risk than I was prepared to take. I had never thought about losing money. After all, we could always make more money. That's what we'd always done. Suddenly, I began to see our long-term security slipping away. I was restless and up at night. I felt so vulnerable and scared.

Arthur: I was actually having trouble breathing. I found myself at times having to pull my car over because I was hyperventilating, and I felt like there was an anchor sitting on top of my chest. I realized I was losing time, concentrating on my investment problems when I should have been focusing my efforts in my area of expertise. When I had the opportunity to work with an experienced financial advisor, I took the leap. This advisor convinced me to revamp my strategy to a much more conservative posture—one that was unfamiliar to me. But I have to admit, I felt so relieved making the change. I never really thought about how hard I'd worked all these years and what it took to accumulate what we both have. We realize now that if we had focused first on not losing what we had, we would never have gotten ourselves into this situation. We'll never make that mistake again.

Even the most intelligent and experienced investors are susceptible to mistakes, especially if they are pulled into the current of the markets and lured by the potential of wealth. It's totally understandable; we've all been in situations where we "got carried away," financially and otherwise. It's up to you to recognize that the first step to financial security is protecting what you have accumulated. Holding on to what you have is a matter of respecting your investments—and by extension, yourself.

Chapter 10

Know What You Want
to Accomplish

"…I just want to make as much money as I can…. I want to retire with the same lifestyle I'm living now…. It would be great if we could pay for both college and graduate school…. I'll probably inherit my retirement fund from my parents…. If I had enough money I could finally quit this job and get into what I really want to do…."

Listening to these common thoughts from investors, perhaps you can recognize how these objectives are vague and unrefined. Where are the numbers? What is the time frame? How can a strategy be developed without the detail needed for the calculations? Yet, this is how many investors select financial products, not realizing they must first fine-tune investment objectives before designing an investment strategy.

You already know the importance of establishing priorities, developing a master plan for your life, and then ranking those priorities so you can live your master plan. Now it's time to talk about the connection between your life goals and your investments. You need to know what you want to accomplish so that you can make wise investment decisions. There is a direct connection between how you invest your money and the lifestyle that can become available to you. In investment language, we call this "defining your investment objectives." There are five generally accepted options:

1. Capital preservation
2. Income
3. Income with growth

4. Growth

5. Aggressive growth

You may be familiar with these already. In some cases, these objectives are presented in terms of risk only, like this:

- Conservative
- Conservative to moderate
- Moderate
- Moderate to aggressive
- Aggressive

Although the main thrust of these objectives may be the same, the choice of phraseology is significant. Descriptors like "conservative" and "aggressive" only tell you about the risk of an investment, not about the anticipated outcome. The phrases we use here identify both the risks and what we are seeking in results.

Let's look at each objective and an example of when it might be most appropriate.

Capital Preservation

Capital preservation means holding on to what you have and not losing it. Michael is a retired investor committed to preserving his capital.

Michael: I've never known much about the whole subject of investing. All I've ever done is work, take care of my family, and put a little money away. I'm 78 now. There are different things that are important to me at this stage of my life. The one thing I know for sure is that if I lose this money, I can't replace it. I've worked hard for what I have. I'm not as concerned with inflation or trying to make more money the way a lot of other people are. If I had to do with less, I would. I would rather know my money is safe. I have to admit that this strategy has resulted in a very low rate of return, but I have to sleep at night. I've made the choice to focus on preserving my capital as my number one goal.

Michael has evaluated his choices and the risks. He knows what he's giving up. He's chosen to take this route and understands he's not beating inflation, and he's not growing his capital. However, there is another factor he hasn't considered here: What if he gets hurt or becomes seriously ill? His wife is deceased. What if he needs some kind of special care he hasn't planned for? He may have to invade his capital to cover those extra expenses—a choice that conflicts with the objective of preserving capital, unless Ed has so much capital that he can afford to make very little on his money and still never outlive his resources.

Income

Income means that your investments produce a revenue stream you can either reinvest or use to live. Lou is a retired physician. He has a quality of life that is very important to him, and he has no intention of giving it up. He is not concerned about leaving any assets to his heirs. His goal is to generate as much income as he can from his investments, including social security, and he's going to spend all of it.

Lou: My children are very successful, and they don't need any financial assistance from me. I've worked in a demanding field of medicine for a long time, and I made plans that I was going to enjoy my retirement. I'm not interested in growing my capital because I don't want to take the risk that comes with that. I'm looking for income, and I'm going to spend all the income from my investments. I'm not concerned with leaving any money to anyone, and I don't have any expectations for extraordinary expenses in the future. This has limited some of my investment options, but I'm more concerned with getting cash flow and getting it now.

Income with Growth

Income with growth means a revenue stream plus opportunities to increase the capital. There's definitely some cash flow from these investments, but here the investor is acknowledging that inflation plays a role in diminishing capital. This is important to consider, especially if you're younger.

Randi is only 56. She has investments from a divorce settlement. Her personal life has been altered dramatically by her change of status. Randi learned the Rule of 72 (described in Chapter 9, "Appreciate the Value of Holding on to What You Have,") while educating herself about handling money. She also learned that inflation has historically averaged a 3% rate. By dividing 3 into 72, she knows that in 24 years she will need twice the money she has now to get the same income in today's dollars. In essence, the value of her money will have been halved.

This means the two million dollars she has will be equivalent to a million dollars in 24 years. Randi is in very good health, and in 24 years she'll be 80. Her life expectancy could be well into her 90s, and she does not want to outlive her resources. She's never worked for a living outside the home and intends to continue to live comfortably. So she needs income, but she also needs to grow her capital. This means she's going to have to take some investment risk because without that risk, she knows she could invade her capital and risk sustainability.

Growth

Growth means capital appreciation, with income as a secondary consideration or not at all.

Scott is an example of someone who's looking for growth. He has a solid employment situation. He's in the financial services business with a unique skill set. His compensation level is very high. He's married and has two young children. He does not need any investment income. There's a lot of stress in his profession, and although he's managed it well, he's concerned about the long-term consequences of staying in this particular field.

Scott: I've recognized I have the potential to make a lot of money. I've been focused on saving as much as I can, particularly early on in our marriage, before we had children. Now that we have children, there are more demands on our finances, and we've had to do some reevaluating. But at present we don't need income from our investments, and we have a long time frame. I know we can be invested for the next 5 to 25 years. I want to take advantage of the options that are available to us. As we age, I know that we're going to have to become more conservative and focus on preserving our capital. However, right now we want to make money, while understanding the risks and coordinating our investment strategy with our life plan, which is to slow down or retire in 20 or 25 years.

Aggressive Growth

Aggressive growth means growing the capital at a more rapid rate, with potentially higher risk, where current income is not a consideration.

Dominic, age 25, is an example of someone who might invest this way. Dominic has recently graduated from college. He's working for the first time in a new job and wants to learn more about investing. He doesn't need any investment income, and he doesn't have any other people to support in his family.

Dominic: I'm very interested in increasing my knowledge of investments. I'll admit that I don't understand a lot about risk. I've never lost money because I've never had money to lose, and of course I'm very young. It's my first time in an exciting new job, and I'm really looking forward to my career. On the other hand, I recognize that if I can save money at a young age and invest with a more aggressive approach, I might get a good jump start and be able to buy a house at an earlier age or even have financial security sooner. My family's advisor of many years tells me that investing takes a long time, and I have to be very patient and not have unrealistic expectations. But I don't need income from my investments, and if I lose the money, I'll just work harder to make up for it. The one thing I have is time.

If you were to illustrate the five investment objectives on a continuum, you would see that the risk elevates as you move through each one. Risk is an important component because there are two sides of the equation to manage: the preservation side and the growth side—or in other words, the risk management (how much can be lost) and the capital appreciation potential (how much can be gained.). Each time you step further up the risk line, you are modifying those parameters. You need to understand the potential consequences of these decisions.

Some investors don't understand the trade-off they make when they choose one of these investment strategies over another. They might say, "I just want growth!" But growth comes with a price. You can't isolate any one of these without understanding the price you're going to pay for making that choice. We'll talk more about the choices and their trade-offs in a later chapter.

Knowing what you want to accomplish helps you understand where your investments are going to fit along this continuum. However, the five objectives alone cannot make your investments successful. You also need other important elements, such as

- Patience
- Time
- The review/evaluation process
- Flexibility

Investing is not like baking a cake. If you've followed a reliable recipe that instructs you to leave the cake in the oven for 45 minutes, when you open the oven, the cake should be done. It could take a little more or less time, and you may need to stick a toothpick in the cake for confirmation, but essentially, you can trust the process every time. That's because baking involves science. Someone has scientifically studied the necessary ingredients, the time frame, the temperature, and other relevant conditions. If you repeatedly follow that strategy for making a chocolate cake, you're going to get a chocolate cake every time.

But investing isn't just science. It's scientific only in part. Let's put aside for a moment those irrational people who open the door at minute 36 and are then annoyed that the cake has fallen or isn't done. Even after you've waited the prescribed 45 minutes, in investing that doesn't guarantee you a completed "cake." As we talked about earlier, having all the right ingredients certainly enhances your probability of creating a superior investment "cake," but many factors that go into making your complete investment "cake" are not in your control. (It is these factors that take investing out of the realm of science.) On top of all the work you've done to align your investment objectives with your master life plan, you still need time, and you still need patience. After you take the investment "cake" out of the oven, you have to look at how you got there and whether you're happy with the result.

Now imagine trying to bake ten of these cakes at once, all with no recipe! This is what's happening to Jack and Dana. Jack describes his profession of 30 years as "exhausting" and says he feels "burned out." He and Dana have five children who span 13 years. Jack has always been opposed to placing all his investment assets with one person, and as a result, they are spread across six or seven locations. Dana knows very little about their investments and has never seen any document that summarizes their assets in a consolidated format. All the advisors have been working independently, and no one advisor knows what assets the others have under their management. Jack prefers it this way. He believes that if he tells too much to any one professional, that person will somehow get control, and Jack won't be in charge anymore. He gives his advisors open-ended instructions, such as, "Just make me money. I want to see results so I can move on to another phase of my life." The advisors have no idea what asset allocations he is using in his total investment picture. They all end up guessing because there's no coordinated effort, even with another professional such as an accountant or attorney. This leads to duplication, higher volatility, higher costs, and poor performance. Jack has been disappointed with his investments over the last few years. He thinks he should have done better, but against what measure and in relation to what priorities? He'll make general statements such as "I'm so sick of working this hard. I just want to take it easy. I want to retire." But he doesn't do the ground work that will take him to that solution, including communicating with his wife. He's uncomfortable trusting any one person or group of people to sit down and do the work up front that is required to get to this answer. As a result, he's convinced he is not achieving his goals and that it is the fault of the advisors because they haven't made him enough money.

How can you avoid being dissatisfied and discouraged in this way? Go through the steps. First, work your priorities. Rank them. Integrate them into your master plan for your life. Query yourself and ask if you are living your priorities. Then look at your investments. Are your investment objectives connected to what you say is important to you? This is a good time to sit down with your advisor and carefully evaluate your current strategy. If your investment objectives are not in line with what you want to accomplish, reexamine your investment direction and bring it into line with the goals you identify as being most important. Focusing your goals with your advisor narrows the investment options that are appropriate and keeps you from digressing.

And remember, you can have more than one objective at a time. You can combine them. Let's say an investor in his late 50s doesn't need income from all his investments, but he'd like to have some income. Perhaps preservation of capital is also a priority, yet he recognizes the need for growth as protection against inflation. In this case, he might be comfortable allocating 30% of his investments to the preservation of capital, 30% to income, and 40% to income with growth. Pure growth objectives would not fit for this investor.

You can interface any of the investment objectives. The only exception might be the two extremes of capital preservation and aggressive growth. It's unusual to see these objectives combined because they have oppositional goals and risk profiles. However, some sophisticated investors will choose this approach if they want to keep cash available, either to do something else or as a hedge against their aggressive position. In financial terms this is known as a "barbell."

Remember, your investment objectives should coordinate well with your priorities and goals, which must come first. The process of selecting investment products is secondary to defining your investment direction and understanding your risk tolerance. Take the time working with your advisor to properly connect your investment strategy to your goals. Stay focused even when the process feels strenuous. Know what you want to accomplish, and you'll significantly increase the probability of success with your investments.

Chapter 11

Be Clear About What You Have and What You Don't Have

This principle of investing—a particularly important one during an economic downturn—doesn't always get the attention it deserves. In the current economic climate, this bears repeating: If you have something, you have it. If you don't, you don't.

As you consider financial independence, you need to carefully evaluate your assets, resources, and goals and then work with your advisor to plan a smooth, strategic entry into your retirement lifestyle. Regardless of how much planning you do, you can be surprised by unexpected results from mistakes, economic downturns, and other unforeseen events that can affect the intended direction. A financial cushion is critical to prepare yourself for unpredictable difficult times that might lie ahead.

Let's take a specific example. Joe and Nancy are married, age 60, with $2 million in liquid assets. They're in relatively good health. They would like to spend about $80,000 a year from their investments. They are anticipating social security and maybe a pension or some rental income to supplement their lifestyle. To earn $80,000 a year on $2 million requires a rate of 4%. That's a reasonable expectation. If this same couple were 35 and wanted to retire and live that lifestyle, it would be unreasonable because the money would have to be managed over many more years. Inflation would eventually eat into the purchasing power of their capital. But at the age of 65, this is a realistic plan.

To achieve these goals, Joe and Nancy need a strategy that will produce cash flow very close to the $80,000. That means that approximately 60% to 70% of this money may be invested in fixed income, and the balance in equities—conservative, income-producing equities. A good rule of thumb is to have in bonds the same percentage as your age in years. This doesn't work for everyone, but it's worthy of consideration. Joe and Nancy's bond allocation of 60% to 70% should consist of high-quality, investment-grade securities. They should be able to spend $80,000 a year from this capital, or about $6,600 a month. At that rate, they will be meeting their goals. They will have what they want to spend, and they will be able to spend what they have.

In addition, if the equities, which make up about 30% to 40% of the assets, appreciate at their average historical rate of return, there may be an additional $40,000 to $50,000 per year added to their portfolio. This will either allow them to draw more money at a future date or provide a buffer when they hit one or more difficult years. That way, regardless of a downturn in the market, Joe and Nancy will have the cash flow they expected from their investments. They will be meeting their goals.

Now let's look at what often occurs. When investors begin investing in an ascending market, they may end up making more money than they expected. Remember, in the preceding example we were counting on a 4% rate of return on a $2 million investment. Let's say in this first year of investing, their investments had a total return of 8% (4% from income and 4% from capital appreciation). They've actually made $160,000, not $80,000. The most prudent plan would be to save the extra $80,000 and spend $80,000 as per the original strategy. Do you think that's what happens? No! There's always something on which to spend that money. It's the roof, it's the garage, it's the refrigerator, it's the car, it's something that the kids need, or it's the vacation. In that first year of healthy gains, Joe and Nancy may need to be reminded, "You are spending your 'rainy-day money.' If you spend it now, you won't have it later!" Imagine knowing that the rainy-day money is being spent while the sun is shining. It's not a good feeling because eventually we are going to hit a bad patch. Usually it takes living the experiences of one of these rough periods to completely understand the consequences of those actions.

Offering financial advice means walking a fine line. On the one hand, your advisor may want to be honest, open, communicative, and also sensitive about your needs and lifestyle priorities. On the other hand, advisors sometimes find themselves feeling like financial bouncers, saying you can't have this; you can't do that. They don't want to say no to you! The best strategy is for you to focus on the annual budget and be clear about your choices. The options you choose must fit within your total financial picture. Your budget may need to be revised. You may benefit from reminders about what you actually have and what you say you want, not only now, but also for the future. Remember, when the future arrives, you won't be able to spend what you no longer have.

Another strategy, too, is for the investors to contribute to the process. I had a discussion with a husband and wife who are retired teachers. Their dream was to retire and move to New York City. They knew they had to do some calculating because New York has a higher cost of living than most cities. Shortly after the economy deteriorated, they called their advisor and said, "We've been doing some thinking. We love our retirement and our lifestyle, and we feel very grateful to you for everything you've done to help us. But we realize that the economy is weakening while we're playing canasta and taking it easy. We're not doing anything critical. So we've thought it over, and we've decided that we're both in good health and perfectly capable. We're going to go back to work. We're going to teach part-time. We'll have some extra income and be less reliant on our investments for our lifestyle. We think it's our responsibility to participate because things have changed, and we can't control the markets."

"Wow," I thought, "what a great feeling, knowing that they were taking responsibility for themselves." They recognized an important reality about investing: You might want to have it, and you think you have it, but if it gets taken away, you don't have it after all. That's a frightening thought. Their idea was to take action now, while they were still capable, to protect the safety of their future assets.

I often wonder about our American culture, where from generation to generation things have become easier for us. We've been lulled into a pattern of wanting to make things less stressful for future generations. Our grandparents, who lived a much more modest lifestyle than we do, wanted to make life easier for our parents. Our parents wanted to make life easier for us, and we, in turn, want to make life easier for our children.

What is the result? It's a chain of systemic enabling! By making life progressively easier for everyone, we have inadvertently unwound the skills people need to be independent! It becomes very difficult to hear the message, "Wait. Stop. If you continue to spend at this rate, you're going to run out of money." It's in everyone's long-term best interest to face this directly. Some investors may hire another advisor who is inclined to give them a different message, maybe a false one, but the one they want to hear. Ultimately, the goal should be to protect you and guide you to the highest possible quality of life based on your standards. At the same time, it is critical for you to understand you can't have it all ways, and together we have to accept the challenging task of facing your options squarely and realistically.

Carol and Leonard, in their early 70s, are a good example of this. They were raised with similar values and have certain feelings about how money should be handled, which you can see from the interview that follows.

Saly: In looking back over the turbulent markets of 2008–2009, do you have a cultural perspective on what happened and why?

Carol: Greed. Everybody wants something; they want it for nothing with the minimum effort. We have developed a society that thinks everything should be available for free. Who asks questions when things are going so well? Do people ask, "Why am I making all this money?" It used to be that if you couldn't pay for it you didn't get it. Now you can just charge your car, mortgage, credit line, and so on. I see people in the food store pull out a credit card, and say, "Oops, this one doesn't work. I'll use another one." I have watched people go through 3, 4, or 5 credit cards.

Saly: You are both in your 70s with grandchildren. What do you remember about your upbringing and the way your family paid for purchases?

Leonard: My father didn't have a credit card until he was in his 70s. Even then he carried one for emergencies only.

Carol: It was always understood that if you had extra money, you put it aside. You saved it, and you never bought anything that you couldn't afford. It's generational. When our kids got married I couldn't believe what they started with: cars, TVs, vacations. We had just a small basic apartment! We were taught to save first and then manage our expenses with what we actually had in our hand.

Saly: As you've gotten older, have you been drawn into some of these newer values about credit?

Carol: We've rarely deviated from those original values. I think we've always been on the more cautious side. When I was a kid, shopping with my mother, and I saw something that I wanted, she would say," I better call Dad first and see if we can do this." I can still remember when Lizzy, our daughter, was 12 or 13 and at the mall with my credit card. She called to ask if she could buy a pair of jeans. I asked, "Why are you calling? You have the credit card!" She said, "They're $60, and everybody is buying them, but I thought I better call you first." We felt very gratified that she was thoughtful and responsible enough to call—and she didn't buy the jeans!

We all can benefit from a lesson in old-fashioned values. Stick to the facts about what you have and what you don't have and construct a reality-based investment strategy rather than one founded on imagined assets or wishful thinking. Although this advice applies to all investors, it may be most difficult for younger investors to accept. You can help break the habit of generational enabling. Be clear about what you have and what you don't have and lead by example.

Chapter 12

Expect to Pay a Price— Either Now or Later— for the Choices You Make About Handling Your Money

Take a moment now to imagine a fantasy for your life. Think about what you want and the way you would like to live. Imagine that you can have all that for as long as you live. Flash to the future and envision your life as you cut back or retire, change your career, or spend more time with your hobbies or your family. In this fantasy, you're going to get a check every month, and you can spend the entire check because the next month there will be a new check. How much money will the check be for?

This is an exercise in understanding the costs of your current lifestyle and projecting how those costs are likely to change in the years ahead. You have to look into the future and estimate how much money you will need to cover your expenses for your lifestyle. In other words, you need to calculate an estimated sum for that monthly check. This exercise can help you plan better and invest properly so that you are more likely to end up with the capital you need in the future.

You can't just look at how much money you spend every year now, multiply it by the number of years to your retirement time frame, and arrive at a total. Remember, we talked earlier about the Rule of 72, that is, how inflation can be expected to erode the purchasing power of money. If your retirement destination is 24 years from now, with inflation you're going to have to double that check (3% rate for inflation) to get to the equivalent result in today's dollars.

It's important for you to have a realistic sense of how much money you'll need in the future so that you can make wise choices now about how to reach that goal. To accomplish that you need a process. The logical nine-step progression described here can simplify the process and specify each calculation you need to make.

1. Estimate Your Desired Income in Today's Dollars

Ask yourself, "If I had all the money I needed to live in the way I want right now, how much income would I need per month?" Answer the question using today's dollars.

Let's say, to use a round number, you would like to have $7,500 per month. Check it out by revisiting the fantasy. Based on your current lifestyle, if you were to receive a monthly check for life, one that you could spend in its entirety and have it replaced at the end of each month, would $7,500 be the right amount?

Remember as you consider this amount that your expenses will change, but you still might want to use today's dollars as a starting point. It's true that you can expect some long-term expenses to go away, such as child care and a mortgage. But some of those costs will be replaced with new expenses in the future, such as health care for yourself or someone you love. To be realistic in making this calculation, you shouldn't modify the amount of money that seems reasonable for you to live on today.

2. Determine Your Time Frame for Financial Independence

While you're still living in the fantasy, think ahead to the day you will be financially independent. This will be the day when you can wake up in the morning and say to yourself with complete freedom, "What do I most want to do today? How do I want to live this day?" Financial independence doesn't have to mean retirement. It could be modifying your work, changing jobs, or realizing your career objectives in some other way. It could mean not working at all and enjoying travel, hobbies, family, or whatever you choose as significant goals for your life. Regardless of your priorities, you should look forward to your "financial independence day."

Now, after you have this picture in mind, how far into the future do you want to plan for this financial independence? Thirty years? Twenty-five? Ten?

3. Adjust the Income Figure for Future Inflation

As a starting point in Step 1, you used the amount of money you would need to live if you were using today's dollars. But in the future, today's dollars won't buy you what they do today. You have to account for inflation.

Inflation is the erosion of the purchasing power of money. Whatever you can buy today for $7,500 a month, you will get a little less of next year and a little less of the year after that, and so on, based on historical patterns of inflation. In other words, you will need more money in the future to buy the same things you're buying today.

For the lifestyle that costs you $7,500 a month this year, next year—assuming a 3% rate of inflation—you'll need 3% more to have the same buying power. For each of the 25 years that lie between the present and your day of financial independence, you'll need 3% more income than the preceding year to keep your purchasing power constant.

Of course there is no guarantee that inflation will stay at 3%. We can use that number because 3% is the average historical rate of inflation. However, that doesn't mean inflation might not be 0% this year and 8% the next year. In 1980, the inflation rate was 13.58%. (www.inflationdata.com)

Contrast inflation with deflation, which also affects your financial future. Let's say you're shopping for a new computer. You look for the best price, and when you see a small laptop on sale, you say to yourself, "This laptop is the perfect size for me, and it costs $2,000. I'm very interested in buying it." If you're in an environment of deflation, what will the computer sell for in a couple of months? It could be less—maybe $1,500. It might even have more functions and still be cheaper. So, you may want to wait. You've probably found yourself saying this about other products, particularly regarding technology. "Why would I buy that camera? There's a better one coming out with more pixels for less money. I'll wait!" Deflation can be momentarily helpful to the consumer, but it is very bad for the economy because people slow down their buying habits and purchase much less. Everyone is waiting. Among most governments, there is great concern about the potential for deflation because it can lead to a stagnant economy. You're not buying, so someone else is not hiring, so you're not getting a job or buying a house, or anything for that matter. This cyclic spiral has far-reaching negative effects.

Inflation is the opposite of deflation. If you're thinking about buying something, and it's likely to be more expensive later, you are inclined to buy it now. Over the years, we can easily reflect on a variety of goods and services that have been dramatically affected by inflation. In 1964, the cost of a movie ticket was less than $1.00. A three-bedroom home was less than $25,000. The average teacher's salary was under $5,000. Things surely have changed! When inflation is present, you continually need more money to buy the same things in the future. Or you will have to buy a little less of what you want because the purchasing power of your money will have been diminished by inflation.

Let's go back now to your monthly $7,500 amount. As you look to your future with that money, you have two choices. You can either expect to keep spending at a rate of $7,500 a month, knowing that over time it will buy less and less, or you can figure out how much more money you will need per month to maintain what is a $7,500 per month lifestyle today. Let's assume you are going to choose the latter. That means you need to know specifically how much more money you will need per month once you adjust for 25 years of inflation. (You may want to reduce the starting figure to accommodate income expected from social security or a pension, but to illustrate this procedure let's use the $7,500 for now.)

Let's assume the average historical inflation rate of 3%. Using that rate, calculate the monthly income you will need 25 years from now to have the same spending power that $7,500 per month gives you today. If you multiply $7,500 by 1.03, you will have the amount needed per month in the second year ($7,725), if you multiply $7,725 by 1.03 you will have the amount needed per month in the third year ($7,957), and so on. You can predict forward 25 years by performing that operation 25 times. (Or let a computer or advanced calculator perform a single operation. Most calculator guide books illustrate financial formulas.) You will see that to preserve your monthly spending power 25 years from now, you will need $15,700. This is congruent with the Rule of 72 (Chapter 9, "Appreciate the Value of Holding on to What You Have"), which would put the 25-year figure just over two times the figure for today's dollars.

The formulas for all the calculations shown in Steps 3 through 8 are shown in the Appendix, "Formulas Used for Chapter 12 Calculations." Some rounding is done here for reading ease.

4. Calculate the Ending Balance You Need to Support the Inflated Income Figure

From Step 3, you now know how much money you're going to need every month to support your lifestyle 25 years in the future. The next question is this: "How much investment capital will I need 25 years from now to support my desired monthly income when I'm ready for financial independence day?"

As you take this step, remember that you may not be spending any of the investment capital itself 25 years from now. It will simply be there to generate interest and capital appreciation sufficient for you to draw your required $15,700 per month. A reasonable assumption is that you can draw an amount equal to 5% of your capital each year without jeopardizing your future.

We know from Step 3 that the $7,500 per month that supports your lifestyle today will have to be about $15,700 per month 25 years from now, which amounts to about $188,000 a year. To calculate the investment capital needed to support your future income of $15,700 per month while protecting the principal, you need to calculate the number for which your expected annual withdrawal of $188,000 is 5%. That calculation is a simple matter of dividing the annual income withdrawal ($188,000) by the withdrawal rate (.05). If you make that calculation, you will find that the amount of investment income you will need 25 years from now is $3,760,000.

We call this figure "Your Number" because it's the total amount of money you have to accumulate if you want to live on the income you've chosen for the future. Don't be intimidated by the size of this number. You will soon see that you can manipulate some of the variables based on your choices. Keep moving through the steps.

5. Estimate Your Starting Balance Using Liquid Assets and Possibly Adding Other Assets That Are Soon to Become Liquid

To assess where you are going to be in the future, you need to account accurately for your current resources. Include only your liquid assets—the true amount of cash and securities you have available. For example, a house you live in should not be counted among your liquid assets because you are not going to sell that house for cash and live in it at the same time. On the other hand, a house currently under agreement to be sold, and settling in fewer than 60 days, can be used in this calculation. You have to be honest about what is liquid and what isn't. Let's say for the sake of our example that you have $250,000 in cash and liquid investments.

6. Estimate the Future Value of Your Current Assets, Using a Rate of Return That Is Realistic Based on Your Investment Portfolio and Asset Allocation

If your asset allocation is 50% bonds and 50% stocks,[1] a reasonable expectation for the rate of return may be about 7%.[2]

---

[1]The 50/50 split of stocks and bonds is an arbitrary choice here, intended to reflect a typical mid-life investor. That ratio may shift with age, allowing young investors to take greater risks in pursuit of long-term gains and older investors to take lesser risks in pursuit of short-term liquidity and security.

[2]Because peaks and valleys are to be expected in the market, the estimate of a 7% return will be more reliable over long periods of time when those peaks and valleys tend to cancel each other out and less reliable over short periods of time that might be dominated by either a peak or a valley.

Using that 7% return rate, you can calculate the value of your liquid assets 25 years from now, building on the $250,000 base of your current liquid assets. If you multiply $250,000 by 1.07, you have the value of your liquid assets in the second year ($267,500); if you multiply $265,700 by 1.07 you have the value of your liquid assets in the third year ($286,225); and so on. You can predict forward 25 years by performing that same operation 25 times (or more easily, let a computer or an advanced calculator do the same thing in a single operation). By now you can see that this is precisely the process you used to calculate inflation in Step 3, except that now you are using total assets rather than a monthly figure, and you are using a return rate of 7% (1.07) rather than an inflation rate of 3% (1.03). You find that 25 years from now the value of your current liquid assets will be $1,356,858.

7. Subtract the Difference Between What You Need for Your Ending Balance and What You Have Now

We call the figure we are about to calculate here "the Gap" because it's the amount of money separating your current assets after 25 years of growth from the ending balance you will want to have at that time. This is the distance you have to make up with your savings rate and with how well you invest those funds. To arrive at the size of your gap, simply subtract the value that you predicted your current investment assets to have 25 years from now ($1,356,858) from the value you will need in your investment assets 25 years from now ($3,760,000). Simple arithmetic predicts the size of your gap to be $2,403,142.

Therefore, your current liquid assets, working for 25 years, will take you a little more than one-third of the way to the investment assets you need at retirement. The money you must save over the next

25 years to cover the shortfall is $2,403,142. That may seem like an insurmountable figure, but let's proceed so that you can understand that this entire process is well within your reach when you apply the variables appropriately to your circumstances.

8. Calculate the Amount You Need to Save Each Year—for Your Designated Time Frame—to Close the Gap and Potentially Achieve Financial Independence

This is the hard reality point of the nine-step process. Some investors may start rationalizing and making excuses, such as, "I think my house is going to be worth a lot more than it is right now." Or "I plan to sell my company for a lot of money. That's a big part of my retirement plan." Or "I'm going to inherit my business from my family, so I'll have plenty of assets." Or "I've had a very successful investment strategy, and I think I can keep doing what I've been doing."

The difficult truth is that it's just too painful to take an honest look at those numbers and then admit that "If I continue on my current course, it's virtually impossible—barring a stroke of luck—for me to achieve my long-term goals." People don't want to do that, so they may run from these harsh facts. But if you want to live the life of financial independence as you have defined it, you need to be honest about the amount of money it's actually going to take and what responsibility you have to make that happen.

To calculate the annual savings needed, you need to divide the gap (in this case $2,403,142) by the most complex figure in this entire process. Don't worry about the complexity of it or even whether you understand it. You don't need to understand this value to have it take you where you want to go any more than you need to understand the physics of flight to have an airplane take you where you want to go. To arrive at the figure to be divided into your gap, you (a) multiply 1.07 (1 plus the rate of return) by itself 25 times (the number of years) to achieve a value of 5.427433; (b) subtract 1 from that value to achieve a value of 4.427433; and (c) divide that value by .07 (the rate of return) to achieve a value of 63.249038. By dividing that value (63.249038) into your gap ($2,403,102), you find that the amount you need to save each year to reach your financial independence after 25 years is $37,995.

At first $37,995 may seem high. You may think, "I can't save that amount of money." But remember, the annual savings figure includes retirement funds with employer matches and perhaps other revenue streams that you can save. Recognize also that you may save less than that figure in the earlier years, but more in the later years as pay raises and cost of living adjustments increase your income substantially over what it is now. Of course the earlier you save, the longer your money can grow, and the higher the probability of achieving your goals.

Let's think for a minute about the extent to which you have additional flexibility within that annual savings goal. The preceding eight steps constitute a system that creates a target you can aim for. This is important because the lack of a target makes inaction likely, and inaction can lead to a lack of control over your future. When you have a target, however, you are free to decide how critically to focus on it. You may conclude that hitting the bull's eye is not crucial to your future happiness, and so over time you might modify your aim in one way or another.

1. You can lengthen your time frame (work a little longer).
2. You can lower your ending balance (live on a bit less per month).

3. You can choose very aggressive investments (but only if you are prepared to take on a higher level of risk).

After you have identified your annual savings target and perhaps made an adjustment or two after reviewing it, you will be ready to take the last step to increase the probability of reaching your personal financial independence.

9. Develop an Asset Allocation Plan

After you complete Step 8, you will have all the data you need to form a strategy:

- The monthly income goal ($7,500)
- The time frame (25 years)
- The monthly goal inflated forward 25 years (about $15,700)
- The ending balance ($3,760,000)
- The starting balance ($250,000)
- The value of the starting balance forward 25 years ($1,356,858)
- The gap between what you will have and what you will need ($2,403,142)
- How much you need to save annually to close the gap ($37,995).

The last step is to develop an asset allocation plan that has the highest probability of helping you achieve your goals. You're asking yourself, "Now that I have a clear financial picture of my future, what investment strategy has the highest probability of resulting in the ending balance I need, given my time frame and resources?"

Investors can get ahead of themselves when they don't give this step careful consideration. They might even bypass this process—call their advisor and say, "I have half a million dollars. What do you think I should do?" The advisor, wanting to be responsive, may suggest multiple investment products that could be suitable. However, the most reliable strategy can be determined accurately only after all the steps have been completed, with or without the involvement of a financial advisor. There are no shortcuts, only short circuits! You need the asset allocation that's right for *you,* based on the facts about you, your goals, and your needs.

Imagine this scenario. What would happen if you called your doctor to say, "I'm having trouble sleeping, and I'd like to talk to you about some drugs for insomnia," and your doctor said, "Oh! I'm so glad you called! I have five drugs right here. Which one would you like to try?" You would be appalled because your doctor wouldn't even have given you a comprehensive exam to determine the diagnosis. How could this professional, with no medical evaluation, recommend any one of five drugs, each appropriate for a different sleep disorder, such as sleep apnea or restless leg syndrome?

You can't solve a problem by grabbing at a solution in the absence of a diagnosis. Because we can be emotional and anxious when it comes to money ("I have to find a solution. I need a solution now!"), and because the state of internal conflict of an unresolved problem is painful, we sometimes compromise the quality of the solution. We want to get the problem behind us. We want to check the box that says "I took care of that!" ("I have an investment strategy. Of course I do.") But only after you've assessed your financial picture carefully and chosen the *right* solution—the *right* asset allocation for you—will you have actually positioned yourself properly for your future. That's the price you have to pay for financial freedom. You need to pay the price of fairly evaluating all your goals and the reality of reaching those goals given your expectations, your time frame, your resources, and what you can contribute. You can reach those goals by making clear choices that can best lead you to the big picture item you wanted: security

Following the nine steps is the right beginning, but there's more. With each decision, you need to make a choice about your money, and you need to pay a price. The price isn't always financial. It can be a price in stress or time, but ultimately you need to pay a price either now or later. Quality of life is measured by more than just money, so these costs should be carefully considered.

Paying Now

How do you pay now? In very simple terms, you can pay now by saving more. That might mean delaying gratification on purchases, trips, or other kinds of expenses. When you put money away for future projects, such as college or graduate school, a vacation home, or your bigger dreams, you're paying now so that you can get something later.

One of the advantages of paying now is that you can develop self-confidence about your ability to save money. There's a feeling of empowerment that comes from taking steps you know can ultimately get you closer to your most important goals. Saving keeps you honest in your dialogue with yourself about what you've committed to do and what is actually happening. The continual harvesting of your income creates a habit that can become familiar to you as you continue to save for your long-term goals.

Another advantage to paying now is that you are aware of current variables, such as tax and inheritance laws. You may have a sense of the current investment conditions, such as interest rates and whether the stock market is historically high or low. All these can change. Tax laws are not in your control, and they can become unfavorable. It would be a shame to find out later that if you had been saving earlier, you might have had the advantage of easier, more favorable regulation. Perhaps you could have saved more money by taking it out of your compensation and also by investing it. Finally, you have the added effect of compounded returns for all the years that your saved money is invested until you need it.

For all these reasons, paying now makes sense. But you have another choice: paying later.

Paying Later

There are some investors who are just not comfortable paying a price now for future goals. Investors whose family members have died at an early age may think they too have a short life expectancy. Investors whose health is not good may think, "I've always wanted to have a vacation home, and I'm not going to wait any longer. I don't see the point in holding out for the future." Investors who feel that they're going to work for a very long time sometimes don't feel they need to save now. They say, "I'm never going to retire. I enjoy what I do, I'm going to work forever, and I'm always going to have income. There are a lot of things I'd really love to do. I'm going to do them now, and if I need something later I'll pay for it then." Investors who expect to inherit large sums may not see the reasoning of a saving strategy. After all, they only have to "wait" until this future event occurs. However, there is no guarantee that the benefactor will still have the same inclinations, or the same assets, to pass to those particular heirs.

Some investors expect an important future transaction, such as an asset sale or their company going public. The expectation that this occurrence will generate a large asset pool mentally substitutes for years of systematic saving.

Similar to paying now, paying later has advantages and disadvantages. One problem with paying later is that you can't be assured of the future. This strategy places a great deal of emphasis on events that are not in your control. In addition, you don't know what other needs are going to come up that might be of a higher priority than those you have presently identified. External factors can also change. What if you run into an unfavorable market, constraining tax laws, health issues, or problems with your job security? If any of these events occur, you won't generate savings the way you thought you could. Another problem is that prices can change over time. You might have your hopes set on a dream house that you're going to pay for later, but by the time you're ready to buy it, the price may have increased to such a great degree that you can't afford it after all. Maybe you thought you would have time to save because what you had in mind was just a modest place in Florida, but by the time you get to that point, that small place was too expensive for your current financial resources. There's a balance that has to go on between what you choose for the future and what you're choosing now.

Let's hear from some investors who have experience in these matters:

Gemma: I remember when we were young children and my parents enjoyed a full-time domestic staff. Whenever we traveled, we took private planes and stayed in lavish resorts. It seemed like every one of our whims was indulged, and money was free to spend. It wasn't until I was a mature adult that I appreciated the extravagance of our lifestyle. My parents had spent much of their money. My dad developed health problems that prematurely shortened his career and his ability to make money. Now my parents have a true need for household help and more customized transportation, but they don't have the assets to afford these expenses.

Bob: I remember when I was a young man in business, working my way through the ranks. I grew up in a poor immigrant household, and we never had much in the way of material possessions. While in the city, on my way to a meeting, I saw the most amazing watch in a store window. It was spellbinding! And yet, I felt it was something I could not afford. I told myself that when I became successful, I would march into that store and buy that watch with no hesitation. For years it was a source of motivation. It sounds foolish now, all this fuss about a timepiece. But for me, it represented something special. Anyway, here's the crazy thing: I did eventually go into the store to buy it, and I couldn't do it! I had delayed gratification for so long, I couldn't actually act on my impulse! Did I not deserve it? Did I not really want it as much as I thought? I had the money and the appropriate lifestyle that went with the watch, so it wasn't financial—or was it? Did my long-established habit of frugality, lingering from my early years, have a hold on me? All I know is, when it came to doing it, I was powerless. And now, 50 years later, it is one of my regrets. I should have believed enough in myself to buy the watch the first time I saw it. I guess the habits we form early in life rarely change, regardless of how much money we have.

Barney: After I left the Navy, I started my career in human resources, working for a large corporation. My wife and I were savers; that habit was instilled in us early on in our upbringing. We were both raised in the Midwest with very conservative values about money and lifestyle needs. We had four children. It was surprising to us when our unmarried daughter became pregnant, with the intention of keeping the child. With mixed emotions, we agreed to support her in this decision, which also included financial support. This added a layer of expense to our long-term plans. Our granddaughter had some special needs, and we financed much of these costs. Sadly, our daughter lately developed some serious health issues, and after desperately seeking various medical alternatives, and using our own financial resources, we lost her. Family is everything to us. Because we had saved so carefully early in life, we had the assets to accommodate a difficult future we could not have foreseen. We needed to be there for those we cared about most. Fortunately, we have a close relationship with our children and grandchildren, so we know we made the right investments!

Lyle: My children were just toddlers, and I was a laborer in my early 30s when my wife just up and said she had had enough of marriage and motherhood. That was the last time I saw her. Imagine trying to raise two sons and work a full-time job when you have no idea what you're doing! This situation was overwhelming, and yet, it inspired me to be a positive role model and provide for my children. I had to make many difficult choices on a daily basis, but I just kept thinking of my family and my strong desire for financial security. Eventually I acquired some of the businesses where I had been employed. I dedicated myself to saving money and learning about investments. It took a while, but when I became successful I provided us with the kind of lifestyle we had always dreamed about. In those early years, I felt guilty often having to say "no" to the kids, but we were barely making it. I had to focus on the bigger picture. Looking back, I believe this experience of delaying short-term gratification contributed to the character of all our family members. I sure am glad I stuck to my plan.

Making the Choice

What do you need now, and what will you need later? Use the answer to that soul-searching question to help you choose when and how much to save. Be honest with yourself about the difference between a necessity and a long-term goal or dream. Think about the extent to which you are willing to save (or pay) now and the extent to which you believe you'll be willing and able to pay later.

What's most important about paying now or paying later is to recognize the choice is up to you. You have to make the choice, commit, and live it. Being disciplined at a young age is a formula for success, even if it takes time for you to be a success in your career choice. If you have followed your life plan, your master plan, and your highest priorities, you'll proceed through a natural transition from where you are now to where you want to be in the future. You're going to make the choices that make the most sense for you.

Chapter 13

Know the Essence of Your Advisor's Brand

What is meant by "brand" in the context of a financial advisor? This does not refer to a mission statement, logo, slogan, product, service, or advertisement. These are all supportive clues, but they are not the essence of the brand. As consumers, we generally think of a brand as a product or service that is almost instantly recognizable. When we're talking about products, familiar brands include Coca-Cola, Kleenex, and Apple. When we're describing service, branding attributes might include VIP standards, or prompt and efficient attention, or outstanding performance. When a brand has developed a consistent history and high level of recognition, it provides comfort to consumers. That brand is reliable, and you can count on it.

Financial advisors also have a brand. You may not even be familiar with this, but it exists. This brand is distinctly reflected in every bit of interaction with the public. It can be summarized best by the advisor's reputation from the client's point of view. Advisors can't be all things to all people, but they can be many things to the most appropriate people. It might interest you to know that every advisor has what is referred to as an "ideal client." It's an imaginary client who's perfect for that advisor in every way. Advisors build their practices by continually seeking additional clients who fit that profile. In other words, wanting to be fair to the people they have already committed to, they establish standards for their practices that define their client populations. These standards optimize their potential to serve their clients effectively. They also need to know what they feel comfortable doing, or not doing, as an advisor. For example, an advisor may not have confidence or experience in complex, illiquid products, such as "alternative investments." This advisor may be concerned with illiquidity and the lack of transparency. But there are other advisors for whom alternative investments may be one of the highlights of their brand.

Conversely, every investor has an ideal advisor in mind, whether they know it or not. The brand you want may not yet be clear to you, but as you spend more time considering different styles and approaches, it's likely the picture of an ideal advisor will present itself. As the investor, it is helpful to have a feeling for what kind of person will be most likely to help you achieve your financial goals. This will be a long-term relationship, so you need to get along very well.

For example, if you wanted to identify the brand for a kind of beverage, you might have brand attributes in mind such as this: "I want something light and not too sweet, not carbonated but with enough vitamins and calories to give me a boost." If you were looking for a new dentist, you might be considering these brand attributes: "I want personalized attention in a small practice, but I want someone from a reputable school so I can be confident in the level of professionalism." Likewise, when you look for a financial advisor, you need to focus on the applicable brand attributes for your investment needs and personal preferences.

> **Meghan:** "I want an advisor who is assertive—who will take control of my financial situation and have a clear sense of what's best for me. I want my advisor to have a vested interest in the long-term success of my entire family."

> **Tim:** "I want an advisor who is patient, respectful, and consistent. I don't want any surprises. I want someone who will take the time to be sure I understand what we're doing with my money."

William: "I want an advisor who is creative and not afraid to take risks. I want someone who is willing to explore all the options with me and challenge the limits of what's possible."

You may not immediately have a clear picture in mind. It may take time to develop an understanding of the brand you want. You may have to interview a number of advisors to get a sense of what is right for you. Here are some of the attributes you may want to consider as you explore and refine the brand that's right for you.

accessible	caring	holistic
adaptable	collaborative	imaginative
articulate	confident	intuitive
assertive	conservative	meticulous
attentive	consistent	nurturing
authoritative	creative	supportive
balanced	friendly	sensitive
business-minded	experienced	wise

With any advisor, there are certain attributes that should be non-negotiable. These aren't so much a part of the brand as they are a foundational requirement. All advisors you consider must be trustworthy. They must have integrity. They must value your money as much if not more than you do. They must respect you.

Ideally, the advisor's brand matches the investor's needs. Interestingly, research has shown that the definition of a brand is in the mind of the recipient. The investor's perception is the true reality. (We talk more about this in Chapter 16, "The Investor's Perception Is the True Reality.") No matter how much an advisor attempts to convey allegiance to a particular brand, your perception and your opinion as to whether it's the brand for you is the most influencing factor. What is important is not just what the advisor says about the brand, but what you hear, accept, understand, and experience.

To assess an advisor's brand, you have to know what that brand is. How can you find out? You have several options.

Option 1: Ask the Advisor Directly About the Brand

What can you expect from your financial advisor? What does the advisor stand for?

Query the advisor on his own brand. This is a perfect opportunity for you to hear the advisor describe his most prominent attributes. As you listen, ask yourself, "When I hear this person speak, do I feel confident? Do I understand what's being communicated to me? What do these remarks tell me about this person's character?" Ultimately, what you are buying from any advisor is judgment. You don't have any way of assessing how this advisor will make recommendations in the future other than to look at what has been done in the past and how well you can assess his brand. Even then, there is no guarantee that the brand won't shift over the years. After all, there's no contract between advisor and client as to what that brand is going to be. It's more of a very, very strong impression played out in actual experience over time.

To some extent, the brand you identify with may be integrated into the investment firm where an advisor is employed. An advisor who works for a large banking institution is likely to differ from an independent advisor who is his own employer. A bank may have policies and restrictions, but there may also be a safety net in a large institution. An independent advisor may have a less restrictive approach but may not have the backing of an established firm. Additionally, when you give consideration to the selection of your advisor, think about where that person is employed and how well that particular organization is going to support the advisor's personal brand. Finally, consider how well that institution's brand independently fits with what you are looking for.

Option 2: Ask Other People About the Advisor's Brand

In a previous chapter I recommended that you get five references from others before you hire an advisor. This provides an opportunity to evaluate the advisor's brand and how well the brand has worked for others. Are those others like you? Can you see yourself working with an advisor who is well-suited to your reference sources?

Option 3: Meet Several Advisors to Compare Their Brands

In addition to getting several references from other people, go and personally check out several advisors. This is especially useful if you don't know the brand you're looking for. Your research may lead you to compare and contrast various brands and business styles. You may discover that certain brands are not the best fit after you have gotten experience searching through a broader selection of potential advisors.

Let's say for example that instead of a financial advisor, you were looking for someone to paint the interior of your house. At first, you might think that the brand of the painter is not critical. Any painter who is cheap and available will do. Absent the awareness of the brand you want, you might hire the first person in the phone book.

Now let's say instead you decide to compare brands. You commit to getting bids from three painters. When the painters arrive, you find that they are very different from one another! You would see by comparing them that you unconsciously had a brand in mind all along. That brand will become clearer to you when you match your mental image of a "good painter" with the painters standing before you. Suddenly, it becomes apparent that you don't just care about fast and cheap; you care about other attributes. Would you feel safe with this person in your house? Will the painter help you choose colors? Does the painter have a relationship with one particular paint company? Could you use whatever paint you wanted? Would the painter work evenings and weekends, and does he have a crew?

You can set up a similar situation by interviewing multiple financial advisors, and you may have to visit with them more than once. Meet a variety of people and notice your reactions. Take notes on the attributes you identify. Look for patterns in what appeals to you and what you find disconcerting. You may not know what brand you're looking for when you start, but you will form a composite of your ideal brand as you gain experience through this process.

Option 4: Recognize and Respect Your Gut Reaction

Our assessments of other people aren't always easily articulated. We may have an impression about someone more than a logical reason for feeling the way we do.

You can set up situations to elicit your gut reaction to an advisor by using "what if" scenarios. Give potential advisors artificial scenarios that could be possible for you and ask them to discuss how they would handle these. "What if this happened to me? How would you handle this? What if I did that? How would you handle it? If this happens, what would you do?"

The answers you get can give you a good idea about the advisors' brands. It can also tell you something about their experience and how they react when things don't go as planned, which may be useful later. Most of all, you can tell from your intuitive reaction if the brand is a suitable fit for you.

Option 5: Know the Brand You Want

Whereas the previous options for discerning an advisor's brand start with learning more about that person, you can also make a determination about a brand by offering clarity about who *you* are. You can give thought to the brand you're after ahead of time, before you ever talk to an advisor. Then when you have this discussion, you can lead the conversation. You can say, "This is what I'm looking for. Are you this or not?" You define the brand, and you present it. Then you can see how comprehensively the advisor can offer what you need.

If you think about it, this is the way we often shop. Let's say you prefer one brand of toothpaste—for example, Colgate Whitening Gel. You can walk into a drugstore and say, "I want Colgate Whitening Gel, and I don't want anything else." If they have all kinds of other toothpastes there but they don't have Colgate Whitening Gel, you might just walk out of the store and go somewhere else because they didn't have what you wanted.

Courage and integrity are critical at this point. You have to have the courage to identify, search for, and locate the brand you need and to recognize when it's just not available in a particular advisor. For their part, advisors also need to be honest and refuse to commit to practices that are in conflict with their principles. A mismatch between what an investor needs and what an advisor has to offer can't be sustained and is best avoided if it's not based on reality.

Option 6: Live It

There's another way to assess an advisor's brand, and that is to live it. When you hire your advisor you can continually ask yourself, "Am I getting the brand I thought I was buying?" And of course there's that other question, "Would I "buy" this person again today? Even if the brand has been stable and reliable, is this still what I need? Do I still want this brand? Or have my needs changed?" Maybe this person has been rock solid, totally consistent, and completely reliable, but you're different than you were years ago. You might want to reconsider whether this advisor can meet your changing needs.

A brand is not personality. It's not how you feel that day. It's not something that someone is trying on. It's not a fleeting idea or a trend. Brand is the very core of what the advisor is representing to the client. When you wake up tomorrow, or next week, or 5 years from now, you need to know that the brand you thought you bought is what you got and continue to have.

It's up to an advisor to develop a personal brand. It's up to you as the investor to do some research to identify the advisor whose brand suits you best.

Chapter 14

Does Your Advisor Care Deeply About You?

Several years ago Richard, a retired executive and widower, made an urgent call to his advisor in the middle of the day. He was calling from the hospital, and he told the investment team that he wanted to speak to his advisor immediately. It wasn't a financial matter, he said, but a deeply personal one. What was so important that it had to be addressed immediately?

It turned out that Richard was in the hospital again because of a reoccurrence of a long-term health condition. He was very sick and deteriorating rapidly. Knowing that he had just a few days to live, he said to his advisor, "This is the last time we are going to speak with each other. I am calling to say good-bye and to thank you for our relationship over the years. I felt respected and cared for by you and your team, and I want to tell you how much that meant to me."

This was clearly an emotional experience for both Richard and his advisor. This story offers insight into the intensity of financial advisory relationships and how advisors and clients can be so closely connected. Like the fortunate people who come to love what they do for a living, the truth is that we should care deeply about our clients, and many of us do. It's up to you to find an advisor who will feel this way about you. This kind of relationship develops over time, but it is important to look for it from the beginning of your search for an advisor.

In studying the relationship between an advisor and an investor, it helps to appreciate the dynamics of the investment markets. When the markets are very strong and the wind is at your back, it's easy to get the impression that investing is purely about buying products. You

might think, "I'll buy this fund. I'll do some trading. I'll do my investments myself. I'll just buy this and sell that." And it seems to work
because most things do when the market is accommodating. When
the tide turns and the market is going the other way, suddenly everything you do is wrong. Investing is no longer so simple or reliable.
Suddenly you desperately need someone to support you, hold your
hand and guide you down the right path. Because the markets change
over time, this flip-flopping between seeing investments as a com-
modity and needing a reliable advisory relationship becomes a perpet-
ual roller coaster. It wreaks havoc on the investor's psyche and detracts
from the larger investment picture. It can be a relief to the client
when the advisor takes the lead in guiding the relationship, although
ultimately both parties participate in the process.

From the start, advisors enter into a sort of "marriage" with their
clients. The relationship goes far beyond investment recommendations. Those are the commodities, but the relationship is not a com-
modity. The relationship is a partnership to which we are fully
committed. As in a marriage, when things get uncomfortable we don't
just quit. We talk about how to make things better. When we have
questions or doubts, we communicate in a constructive dialogue to get
ourselves to a better place.

The more difficult the markets are, the more important it is to
know that the stability of the relationship with your advisor is
unshakeable. When everything around you that you've ever relied on,
read, gotten advice on, or lived is all unraveling, you discover the one
thing you must know for sure: Your advisor is going to give you the
very best advice available because he or she is committed to your welfare and the protection of your family. For advisors to deliver at that
level, they have to have a deep, caring relationship with their clients.

This can be hard for some investors to understand, especially if they don't know how their advisor feels about them as clients. Sometimes the advisor doesn't know how the client feels, either. Just as in any relationship that continues for long periods of time, we can become complacent. Both the investor and the advisor can make assumptions about the relationship. The unstated implication is, "We've been together 15 years; what do you want me to say? You want me to tell you I care about you? I'm still here, aren't I? Of course I'm happy with you. Otherwise I would have left, right?" But to assume the mutual value and stability of a relationship is different than to tell someone how you feel.

To tell someone how you feel is to actually say the words.

- I care about you and your family, and I am so pleased to work with you.
- I appreciate the way you're putting your best foot forward.
- I'm so glad that we have a mutually collaborative relationship.

Do you see how these statements can be made by either investors or advisors? The communication is two-way. If it's hard to use this language, an easier way to say it is to share what you appreciate about the other person, such as, "Do you know what I admire about you?" Or "I enjoy you so much, because…." Or "Do you know what's great about our relationship?" These are all unofficial ways of telling people you care deeply about them.

In business, we've gotten away from the concept of sharing at this emotional level. Are we afraid of appearing too vulnerable or sentimental? The truth is that this is an opportunity to remind others we are human! Everyone wants to feel cared about or needed, as long as the feelings are genuine. Even if we are not comfortable with the word "love," we can still find suitable language, like "I want to tell you how much I value our relationship and how much I enjoy working with you."

When investors thank their advisor for advice, the advisor should respond that it is a pleasure and a privilege to serve them. Words of thanks from an investor are not just about helping to put their kids through college or to improve investment performance. They're thanking the advisor for the advice, guidance, and commitment. Every chance an advisor gets, it's important to thank our clients, too—not only for their business, but also for the relationship. This is the kind of mutual respect and appreciation you and your advisor should feel for each other.

As an investor, when you look for a long-term relationship with an advisor—someone who is going to work with your family; maybe your parents, your children, your accountant, your attorney—that search should have in its standards someone who is going to genuinely care about you. You need an advisor who has the courage to talk about devotion and practice it in professional relationships.

Sometimes this kind of all-or-nothing relationship with an advisor can bring up fears in investors' minds about having their investments with one person. I've asked investors why they feel comfortable having their investments with one advisor. Nathan, a retired entrepreneur, explains his feelings about his advisor:

Nathan: I know from experience when I work with one trusted advisor, I benefit from a comprehensive strategy. It's not fragmented, and I don't have to worry about conflicting parts. Administratively, everything's in one place and I know exactly how I can find the pieces. If there's a problem, it's easy to track it down because there are only so many options for how it could have occurred. In terms of costs, I know I'm getting the best pricing because I'm benefiting from the aggregation of all my assets and the cost advantages that accompany that. In addition, I know the investment firm thinks highly of me, because I'm a bigger fish. With all my assets at one location, I can be more important, more present, and when I need something, my advisor is in a better position to obtain that for me.

Of course, we have a close relationship that extends back over 25 years. And it's been very hard for me to have faith in people. I had a tumultuous upbringing, and everything I saved and invested was a function of my learning to count on myself and no one else. In my family life, in my business, there are very few people in the world I feel I can trust. That trust has to be earned.

The following interview with Marcy and Ron, (retired, in their early 70s) says more about this subject.

Saly: Looking back at 2007–2008, what do your friends say about what they may have done wrong with their investments?

Ron: The most common mistake is that they placed their investments with the wrong person and did not pay enough attention to what was happening.

Saly: Did they not know enough about the character of that person, or their investment philosophy, or investments in general?

Ron: They didn't know how to evaluate risk, and they didn't do enough research on the advisors they hired. They were completely focused on the big returns, and at 60 years old found themselves 100% in equities. How many years were so good that people thought the bubble was never going to burst?

Ron: You can't cherry-pick in advance the years that are going to be great and then somehow know that the tide is turning the other way. Our advisor said from the beginning, "It's not what you do when things are good, it's how you get through the tough times." That is what we considered when we decided to find one person to handle everything.

Saly: What was the impetus that contributed to your seeking a specific advisor?

Marcy: We were handling all our investments ourselves, using the S&P index as a standard, but we felt very uncomfortable when we started to accumulate some money. We didn't know anything about it and wanted someone else to take care of it. But I also was afraid to rely on one person. It was very difficult to feel I was giving up the control, even though I did not feel competent myself.

Saly: So somewhere along the line you overcame that emotional hurdle. You no longer think, "Oh my, our investment assets are all with one person."

Ron: I was more nervous in the beginning. I'm not now. We talked to four or five potential advisors to get different perspectives, and we knew people who knew each advisor. One in particular seemed to have a firm grasp of our needs, and the chemistry felt right.

Marcy: We had to arrive at a feeling of comfort. I remember when we first spoke. Later, I said to Ron, "I don't know if this advisor is going to accept us, but I am going to tell you right now, she is going to tell you like it is, and you are going to listen to her. That's the way she works. You are going to have to decide if you can live with that." But when we walked out of the office, we both agreed, "That's it; she's the one."

Saly: So if other people say they are thinking about hiring an advisor, and they ask for your advice, what would you tell them?

Marcy: I would tell them to see people that are either living the way they want to live or intelligent enough to trust, and learn who advises them. Find five or six advisors, and talk to them at length. Look deep into their character. I think it's a very personal kind of thing. The relationship with the advisor goes far beyond money, and it should not be underestimated. You are not buying an investment, you are buying a life partner. You are investing in a person first.

Ron: You need some sense of what's happening, and if you don't, you need to speak up and say you don't understand. Ask to have things explained in another way. But make sure you continue to watch what is going on and keep communicating with the advisor. Meaningful relationships can endure all kinds of experiences, but you have to stand up for yourself.

Even the successful relationships have to weather difficult circumstances. The following interview with Sam and Madeline, a married couple in their early 60s, illustrates this point.

Madeline: I remember the late 1990s, when the markets were skyrocketing, especially the NASDAQ. People we knew were making crazy returns, 50%, 100%, 150%! It seemed like we were being left out.

Sam: It was frustrating to watch all our friends make money so quickly, and yet our strategy was so conservative. I felt like we were being held back from participating. When I challenged our advisor about this, I was reminded we had a specific investment strategy that limited our risk, particularly to small cap stocks. Our advisor insisted the returns in the Internet stocks would not continue, and there was a good chance they would reverse. At the time, I was disbelieving and even resentful of this outlook.

Madeline: We considered replacing our advisor. We began to doubt our strategy and wondered if this was the right person for us. Maybe we were losing an important money-making opportunity. Perhaps, we thought, our advisor was imposing too much of a personal bias about investing onto our strategy. After all, it was our money, and we were the decision makers.

Sam: Then in March 2000, things started to blow up. All of a sudden the NASDAQ swooned, and our friends stopped talking about their investment successes. We watched the markets go down dramatically, more than 45% over the next 2 years.

Madeline: It was hard to face, but we realized that if we had followed our instincts and gone along with our friends, we would have lost an enormous amount of money.

Sam: Previously, in the late 1990s we had resisted when advised to reduce our equities and increase our tax-free bonds. After the financial pullback of 2000–2002, we realized that this strategy helped us minimize the damage to our investments. At the time, it was hard for me to get the words out, but I remember ultimately thanking our advisor for protecting us from ourselves!

Madeline: Our advisor felt secure enough to push back at us when we were on the verge of making a poor investment decision. Being in a close partnership means you have to feel safe, offering and accepting criticism, while knowing that you are not risking the underlying relationship. In fact, you are protecting it.

All this caring may sound appealing, but how do you, the investor, go about getting it? How do you find an advisor who will be the right match for your needs? It begins with making the search a priority, and that means the commitment of time and attention. This is not a family vacation; this is your life! The following guidelines are designed to help you focus on finding an advisor who will give you the care and quality you need.

1. Begin by collecting a list of names from friends and other advisors. Research the advisors' backgrounds on the Internet and on the Financial Industry Regulatory Authority website www.finra.org.

2. Make appointments to communicate and meet directly with the lead advisor on each team. If possible, eyeball that advisor to get a feeling for interactive style and body language. What does your intuition tell you about the prospects for this "match?"

3. Get to know the entire team, including support personnel because they will be your first line of contact in the practice. Do they treat you with respect and make you feel special? Can you tell that the relationship will be important to them?

4. Get a proposal, in writing! I can't tell you how many times I have seen people contemplate critical investment decisions without getting anything in writing. The best way for an advisor to "show the love" is to produce a written strategic plan. This illustrates that the advisor understands your most important life issues and will make a commitment to helping you to achieve your long-term goals. The proposal should be simple and straightforward. If the advisor uses investment managers, mutual funds, or other investments with audited results, the proposal should include a performance history of at least 5 years. You should commit to understanding it, particularly with regard to risk and costs.

5. Inquire about the performance review process because it should be no less than semi-annual. Obtain a copy of a sample performance report and make sure you can interpret the information in a way that has relevance to you.

6. Have a clear agreement about the communications process. Does the advisor use a contact management system to keep you periodically informed? Will the advisor interface with and assist your important family members, such as your spouse and children? What kind of access will you have in addition to the office phone number, such as email addresses, and the advisor and team members' cell phones? When you contact the advisor after hours, what will be the response time, and is that acceptable to you?

7. Ask the advisor to discuss his or her relationship with the firm and with the respective management. What is the longevity with a particular firm and the rationale for remaining there? How well are the firm's brand and values aligned with the advisor's? How strong is the advisor's commitment to the investment industry, and will that serve your time frame? Is there a solid succession plan for the team?

8. Ask for at least five references, such as three existing clients (whom the advisor must contact first to obtain permission), one CPA, and one attorney. Query them about the advisor's business style and character.

Because the client/advisor relationship can take on great importance in your quality of life, it is deserving of the same kind of research you would invest in your education, career, and marriage or partner. Time and effort invested early on can get you much closer to finding that special advisor with whom you can have a mutually rewarding relationship. Don't give up until you know in your heart that this is the person and team that work best for your needs.

Of course we must accept that all partnerships go through highs and lows. What you must realize is that these low periods are not entirely negative. They can serve a legitimate function by revealing the nature of the advisor/investor relationship in ways that the highs cannot. They present opportunities to improve communication and enhance the relationship. Because these difficult periods are inevitable, we should be prepared to take advantage of their potential to serve as little "tests." An advisory relationship with solid footing should emerge resiliently from a setback and find greater strength.

Chapter 15

Expect to Be Taken Care Of

By now you may be warming up to the possibility of pursuing and selecting an advisor who is truly committed to you and your investments. What is the potential for the extent of that commitment? It can be more than you think. The following stories illustrate how that commitment can be lived in reality.

Anthony: We were in Europe on vacation. My wife and I were in Prague at the airport waiting to come home. Suddenly I felt faint and had a seizure just as we were about to board the plane. My wife was frantic because I was incapacitated. We were in a strange country far from home. She didn't know what to do. Her first reaction was to call someone who had always been there for us, our family financial advisor. The advisor arranged for me to be flown to Vienna where I was admitted to the hospital. It turned out I had a medical problem that required immediate attention. Several weeks later, after my recovery, my wife and I flew home. We had planned our trip so that we could attend our son's wedding shortly thereafter. My wife said, "If I hadn't gotten you out of there, I'm not sure you would have made it to the wedding or made it home at all." When we thought things over, we noted that the person we chose to call first in a family emergency was the person who handles our money. But that's the kind of relationship we've always had with our advisor.

Elaine: I graduated from culinary school and was fortunate enough to win the lottery in my small town. I didn't know anything about investments, and a friend referred me to her financial advisor, whom I promptly called. After all, I wasn't used to handling this kind of money. My first goal was to travel to Italy so I could learn more about Tuscan cuisine. Within an hour of arriving, my wallet was stolen. Of course all I could think about was what might happen to my identity and this lottery money. I called my financial advisor long distance and got my card blocked and money wired to me. My identity was protected, and in no time I had cash. Ultimately, I had a wonderful trip. This situation could have been horribly destructive to my whole life, and yet with one phone call I got an instant response and the urgent help I needed.

Judy: In the mid 1980s, my husband Harry learned he had late stage pancreatic cancer. Our children were young—in their teens. It was devastating for all of us. We knew Harry had a very short life expectancy. My cousin had been working with a financial advisor, and he spoke highly of her. She immediately traveled to our home to meet with us. Together, we had a family meeting. It was very intense, and we knew she would have only one or two chances to actually communicate with Harry.

When the advisor arrived, Harry was lying on the couch, immobile. After a brief conversation of introduction, he turned to her with great seriousness and said, "Look, I don't know you. All I know is that you work with my wife's cousin. I'm just going to tell you up front: I need somebody who's going to take care of my family. I'm not going to live long, maybe a couple weeks. We've already done all our crying. I have three teenage kids. They're going to need guidance and someone to offer solid advice. I need to know you're going to be committed, and you're never going to abandon my family. We're not just hiring you to be our financial advisor, we're hiring you to be our family advisor and to stand by us. When my kids grow up, when my wife needs you, I need to know that you're going to be there for them. We need to make a pact together, so when I die I will know in my heart that you are the right person and you're going to fulfill this commitment." Howard made our new advisor promise she would take care of our family, no matter what. Now my children are grown and live all over the country. One daughter lives in North Carolina and is a professional caterer. Our son, a successful lawyer, lives in Washington, DC. He is married to a film producer, and they have three children. Our other daughter lives in Rochester, NY, and she's a physician. I still live in that same house where we met on that day years ago. Our advisor has honored her commitment to our family and has been with us every step of the way.

What can we learn from all these stories? Your financial advisor, like no one else, can serve as a trusted resource to you and your family that goes way beyond your money. Your financial advisor should think of you as someone who is so valuable that you must be cared for and vigilantly protected. It's about so much more than the money.

When you work with a focused financial advisor, everything about you and your family becomes the center of interest. Are you healthy? Are you happy? Do you feel secure? What is your family situation? Do you have something you love to do? Do you enjoy your career? How would you rate your quality of life? The financial advisor should attend to you as a whole person because there's no point in helping you to achieve great accomplishments financially when underneath it all, you're miserable. That doesn't mean a financial advisor is qualified to solve problems outside investment expertise, but in whatever way the financial advisor is knowledgeable and can be supportive, that should be coming through to you as an investor. However, being taken care of does not mean you are free to abdicate your responsibility, either. There is a delicate balance between what the advisor does to care for you and what you do to care for yourself.

Your money reaches into every area of your life. Think back to your list of priorities. Health. Family. Financial security. Fun and recreation. Career. Philanthropy. What other one professional has an intimate knowledge of your life as a whole—in every area, in the past, present, and even your hopes for the future? Your financial advisor has a unique perspective on you that almost no other professional is likely to have. Your financial advisor should not be interested in just your money, but also in your financial security, your happiness, and the safety of your family.

You might not be prepared for that kind of relationship with your financial advisor. You could say it doesn't interest you for your advisor to be involved in the bigger picture of your life. Perhaps you see your personal life as none of the advisor's business. Different financial advisors approach advising with varying points of view. If you want a financial advisor who's going to treat your whole family, look at the scope of your whole life, and be attached to and committed to your life goals, that's one particular type of advisor. If you want someone who's going to be occupied with just the numbers, that's a different type of advisor.

A word of caution: Even if you choose an advisor who will attend only to the financial aspects of your life—in other words, when it *is* just about the money—you'll still expect quality advice that reflects the advisor's commitment. I know one 96-year-old gentleman, Bruce, whose advisor suggested he buy small cap stocks. Bruce might never see the gains on that kind of investment. Did this advisor have a true commitment to Bruce's needs and goals?

Katherine, an unsophisticated, risk averse investor in her late 50s, lost more than half of her investments in speculative high-yield corporate bonds. When she recognized what was happening, she called her advisor for advice and information. She was assured that everything was "fine," and that it "would all work out in a few years," and she should "be more patient and wait it out." Does Katherine's advisor understand her goals and risk tolerance? How well does this investment strategy and subsequent response illustrate a true commitment from the advisor?

How do you know you're hiring an advisor who will invest in you as much as you're investing in that relationship? First, you have to recognize what's important to you. Second, you have to ask for it. Third, you have to know if you're getting it.

Recognize What Is Important to You

Do you want an advisor who will take care of you as if you're part of the family? Do you expect to be taken care of? If you do, be honest about it. If you don't, then define what you do want in an advisor. Maintain a high standard and don't settle for anything less.

In Chapter 13, "Know the Essence of Your Advisor's Brand," you were given the steps for finding an advisor. I suggested you compare advisors, interview their teams, and get proposals in writing. That is Part One in the process of finding the right advisor. Part Two is to sit down at length with the advisor you've identified. Your interview process should include questions that can help you know more about the nature of the relationship and whether it's the right relationship for you. If you already have an advisor, you can conduct an interview using the questions in the next section as if you were starting the relationship for the first time.

Ask for It

Here are some interview questions I suggest to help you formulate your expectations.

1. To what extent will we talk about my life plan and long-term priorities?

2. How will you help me to assess my current investments and make a plan going forward to identify the best strategy?

3. How does your business conduct reflect a long-term commitment to my personal and financial welfare?

4. How often should I be looking at my investments? How often should we evaluate them together?

5. What assessments should we be using?

6. How do I know you're thinking about our whole family picture and not just the numbers?

7. How do I know you are keeping in step with our evolving goals?

8. How much time can I reasonably expect to have with you to discuss our goals and our progress, and how frequently will we conduct these reviews?

9. What are we going to do when the strategy is not working in accordance with the goals we established together? (Here, you can provide some examples that may be applicable to your situation.)

10. What is your vision for our relationship in 20 years?

These are the kinds of questions you can ask to assess the likelihood that you're going to be taken care of as if you're part of the family. We've talked throughout the chapters about the answers to some of these questions, so you have a sense of what you should want to hear. For example, you already know you should expect a scheduled performance review. You know you should be able to interpret the information in your financial reports. If you don't get the answers you need from your advisor, then you need to make a change—either by redesigning the relationship with new expectations or by choosing a new advisor who will take an interest in you to the degree that you expect.

When you have had all these questions answered to your satisfaction, and when you have defined the relationship and appropriate expectations, you're likely to have found the advisor you need. Don't lose faith; the ideal person for you is out there! Don't compromise in your search or in your principles for what you know you and your family deserve.

Know If You Are Getting It

When you're comfortable with your advisor, you can start to work together to meet your financial goals. Remember to periodically assess whether you are continuing to be taken care of as you had anticipated.

In Chapter 13 we talked briefly about a little "test" we use to evaluate investments and also people. Look at your investments and ask yourself if, knowing what you know now, you would buy them again. If the answer is no, then you may need to sell them. The same applies to your relationship with your advisor. Ask yourself, knowing what you know now, would you hire this person all over again?

This opens the door to a potentially difficult situation. What if the answer is no? Sometimes investors don't want to confront the real answer to that question. They don't want to accept that they might have to fire their advisor. It's too painful, so they make excuses. They think, "I'll do this and then maybe it will work." They make machinations instead of just dealing with the problem, which is "If I had known then what I know now, I would not have hired this person today. I made a mistake. I hired the wrong person."

To be fair to your advisor, you have to go through this process again. Even if in your gut you're thinking, "I feel I hired the wrong person," you should repeat the process of interviewing the advisor within the existing relationship. You can sit down with your current advisor and ask questions as if you're a brand new client. At this point it is critical that you communicate candidly about your expectations and needs. This is a perfect opportunity to explain how you feel about the partnership. For the relationship to survive and flourish, the advisor must understand your needs and be prepared to address them to your satisfaction.

Drew had this kind of experience with his longstanding advisor.

Drew: I had been working with my advisor for more than 20 years. We have had what I've considered to be a successful relationship. But 9 years ago, we had a pretty serious blip that almost caused us to part company.

In the very profitable markets of the 1990s, I made a lot of money. Believe me, I had no complaints! I thought my advisor was doing a great job. In early 2000, the markets had a pretty serious regression. I lost some money, but I didn't think much of it. My advisor counseled me that it was probably just a run of the mill "pullback" and I should be patient. Later that year, and continuing well into 2002, there was another very severe corrective phase, in which I lost about 25% of my assets. My money was divided between stocks and bonds, and the bonds did very well. However, I was very unhappy with the performance of my stock holdings. I felt that they should have held up better, and my risks should have been minimized. Some of my stock investments persisted in doing worse than the S and P 500 index, and that is the benchmark I have always used to measure my performance.

In May 2002, in a state of total frustration, I called my advisor, and I insisted we meet to discuss what happened. I was disappointed with the events over the past 2 years, and I had second thoughts about the relationship. I lost my temper at times, and our conversation didn't go smoothly. But in the process, I learned I hadn't been as clear as I could have been about my expectations and the rules of engagement between us. My advisor and I had taken too much for granted and become complacent in our communication. I had to take some responsibility for what was happening. It wasn't all my advisor's fault.

This meeting was cathartic for both of us. When I got my emotions under control, I could articulate more clearly what I needed in our relationship. My advisor then had the opportunity to acknowledge what was realistic and obtainable. Not only did we develop a new strategy, but we also agreed to restructure the way we communicated with one another. This meant changing the frequency, the quality, even the semantics of our discussions. Before this epiphany, I had concluded that the relationship should be terminated. After the meeting, I realized this setback actually provided an opportunity to convey my expectations and help my advisor to better understand my needs. We agreed we needed to be more collaborative and sensitive to each other's perspective.

Through the most recent market correction, my advisor and I have handled things so much better. Our relationship has reached a new level because we made the most important investment—in ourselves! With the benefit of hindsight, I think investors should meet with their advisors annually to review the actual advisory relationship, separate from the investment performance. Just as an employee and employer might go through an annual review process, I think it is valuable for investors and clients to have a similar kind of discussion. I believe if I had been doing this on a regular basis, we would have avoided much of the stress, concern, and subsequently painful dialogue that ensued for both of us. Ultimately, however, I learned a great deal from the experience. And, most important, I appreciate the value of what it has created for both of us. That is why I feel confident in the longevity of this relationship.

Chapter 16

The Investor's Perception
Is the True Reality

As we've been talking about your advisory relationship and the ways in which your financial advisor can help you achieve your goals, there's a critical point to remember. When it comes down to it, the money is yours, and you're in command. No matter what the choices are or what an advisor encourages you to do, as the investor you have the final say. Your perception is the true reality.

You might have conflicting feelings about being in charge of your money. There's a part of this reality that may feel scary and out of control. Particularly if you're not confident in your investment knowledge, you might think, "I don't want to be in charge!" You might want someone with more expertise to make the decisions and keep your money safe.

On the other hand, it can be very empowering to realize that no matter what, you are the ultimate decision maker when it comes to your money. Either way, taking full ownership of your investment decisions is a huge responsibility. You are in charge. If you abdicate the responsibility to someone else, then your money is at risk and it's your fault. You need to assert yourself and accept accountability.

You must learn enough to be confident in your investment decisions—both the ones you make on your own and the ones you make in collaboration with your advisor. When knowledge or confidence is lacking, you must stop yourself from making significant financial decisions. Even if someone tells you an investment or a decision is the way to go, if you don't understand it you should forego the opportunity because *your* perception is the true reality. Someone else's perception

151

is irrelevant. Listen to your own voice. A decision is right only if it's right for YOU.

What happens when you have a relationship with a financial advisor, and you know you're not fully educated about the recommendations you're getting? Perhaps you feel you're not sure of what your advisor is saying. All you have is a gut reaction, either positive or negative. Let's say, for instance, your advisor is making a recommendation that instinctively makes you uncomfortable. At this point, you have two choices. On one hand, you may be tempted to say to your advisor, "I'm sure you're right. I'm not comfortable with it, but it's probably because I don't understand it. Let's do it your way." On the other hand, you might say, "I know you think this is the right way to go, but I'm just not sure, so I'm going to say no." Which way is right?

Whenever you find yourself in this situation, remember, it's your perception that counts. If you feel uncomfortable with a decision but you're not sure why, it's a sign that you are lacking the understanding you need at that moment. To move forward and take responsibility for the decision, you need to consider a third option, which is to interrupt the process. You can say to an advisor, "I need to stop you here. We need to find a way for me to understand this concept before I can make a decision."

It's not always easy to do this. You may feel like you're questioning your advisor's expertise, and you don't want to be intrusive. You can overcome this hesitation by sharing your point of view. It might sound something like this: "I know you want what's best for me. This isn't about your intentions. This is about my becoming a more informed consumer and understanding risks. And I have no idea what you're talking about! I need to find out more before I can make this decision."

It's humbling to admit that you don't understand a recommendation. You might think to yourself, "My advisor has explained this concept to me a thousand times, and I still don't get it." You may start to question your own intelligence and wonder if the problem is coming from your own lack of knowledge or your unfamiliarity with the specifics. But it can just as easily be the other person, who may not have the skills to explain it well or who may not be listening intently to your concerns.

An outstanding financial advisor is a dedicated listener. This means hearing what you say and also "hearing" what you don't say. Your advisor should take the time to know you well and identify signs that you are feeling stressed, uninformed, and afraid to express your opinion. For example, an experienced, thoughtful advisor can recognize when clients are uncomfortable just by their body language, voice intonation, and facial expressions. Folded arms and legs, and leaning back, can be signs of hesitation. Some investors may lose the rhythm in their speech, furrow their brow, or show a loss of confidence in their word choices and the direction of the conversation. Overall, they may just look uncomfortable, as if they are suddenly in tight-fitting clothing.

The attentive advisor learns the patterns of the investor's voice and moods; by the time the greeting "hello" is uttered, the advisor knows whether there is something weighing on the client's mind. An advisor needs to be sensitive to your cues and say, "I'm getting the feeling something is bothering you. Can you tell me what you're thinking right now?" This gives you the opportunity to express what you don't understand or what you find discomforting. Then the advisor knows how you feel and can address your concerns directly. The advisor can't think or talk for you; communication has to come from both sides. However, the advisor can be a meaningful facilitator when you need support and offer you the safety net of a relationship in which you can openly express yourself.

As an investor, you need to recognize these same signs *in yourself*. If your advisor doesn't recognize your hesitation and inquire about it, then you must. Learn the signs of your own discomfort. Be aware of your own body language. If you're making faces, crossing your limbs, and feeling a twinge of discomfort, that's when you should alert yourself and say, "I need to know more." Pay attention to those signals because they are valid, and you must advocate for yourself.

When it comes to finding the right balance between the expertise of your advisor and your own knowledge as an investor, think about the analogy of a doctor/patient relationship. Your doctor may have extremely specialized and highly technical experience. Many people put their health in the hands of their doctors, trusting that they know best and will give them the right advice. But just as with your investments, you are in charge of your health. If something doesn't feel right to you, and you don't speak up, you could be putting your health in jeopardy. Your doctor needs to know how you feel to help you make the right decisions.

Let's say your doctor tells you that you have a serious medical condition, and he needs to take aggressive action now, either surgery or medication, or both. You could just put the decision in the hands of your doctor and agree. But what if that choice isn't right for you? You could take the decision out of your doctor's hands and say, "No, I'm going to wait." But what if waiting makes the condition worse? The best option is to communicate with your doctor, as difficult as it may be, and to realize that despite the doctor's expertise, it's your body and he needs to include you in the decision. Despite your knowledge of medicine or lack of it, you need to realize it's up to you to become better educated. You have to find out about all kinds of treatments, get other opinions, and ask for the tests you need to move forward with confidence and peace of mind. Even if the only impetus for taking these measures is a gut reaction that something's not right, you need to stand up for yourself and say, "I know as my doctor you're the expert. But it's my body, and I need you to do this for me. I'm the patient, and my perception is the true reality."

This medical analogy can be applied to your investments. It's your money. To be confident in your decisions, you need to take the time to learn. Advisors generally agree that in the long run, an educated and informed client is a better decision maker.

What happens if you don't make this investment in yourself? Janis is an investor who had this experience.

Janis: I know I'm not an expert when it comes to money. I see myself as a real novice. But I wanted to learn, so I joined a wealth management program to see if I could expand my knowledge about investing. As part of this program, the people who were participating were invited to take part in various investment deals—private opportunities such as investing in a start-up business or buying into a real estate investment with other people.

My husband and I were feeling financially confident at the time, and we thought it would be a good time to experiment with some of our investments and try some new things. We bought shares in a real estate investment, a gas and oil partnership, and a pharmaceutical start-up company. We invested small amounts of money—the bare minimum we could contribute and still participate so we could learn how to do it.

And we did learn! We learned a lot about the process of investing and how these deals can work. But unfortunately, we also learned that we knew even less about investing than we thought! Only one of the investments has turned out to be reputable, and it remains to be seen how that one will end up. But in the other two, we lost most of our investment. We wrote checks to people we didn't know and didn't necessarily trust. We invested in products we didn't fully understand. We'll probably never see that money again.

And the thing is, I knew it all along. From the beginning, I had this weird feeling that we were all acting like lemmings going off a cliff. But the information seemed so reliable, and the advisors seemed so sure about what they were talking about; it was easy to just throw up our hands and say, "Hey, these people know what they're doing, and we don't, so let's try it." The fact that other smart, educated, sophisticated investors that I trusted were also participating in these deals encouraged us even further. This just goes to show we were in good company in our naïveté.

Saly: Why didn't you stop yourselves in the process and say, "We don't know enough about what we're doing?" At a minimum, that seems like something you would have noticed and addressed.

Janis: It does! My husband Steve and I might not know a lot about investing, but we're not reckless with our money. I suppose one thing that held me back from getting involved was my own self-doubt. After I'd asked the same question a dozen times and been given more and more extensive information, I guess I felt like I needed to stop asking. I should have taken my confusion as a clue that the investments weren't right for us.

Janis' experience illustrates that it's easy to forget that you are in charge of your money. To take responsibility for your investments, you have to tune into your needs and make sure they are addressed. Peggy talks about how she does this now with her accountant—a process you can easily use with your advisor.

Peggy: I've learned to trust if I can't actually say the words and explain a concept, then I don't actually understand it. In areas where I don't have a lot of expertise—like with my doctor, my attorney, and my accountant—whenever they explain a situation to me, I make sure I can competently restate it until they say, "Yes, you've got it right." If they can't say that, then I'm still missing some pieces, and I won't make an important decision until I fully understand. I've learned to trust that just because I don't understand something doesn't mean the problem is necessarily me. It may be the other person's inability to explain the situation more clearly, or simplify what I don't understand. In some cases, I've discovered it's actually because the other person doesn't understand it all that well! It takes time for me to go through this process, and I often go to outside sources to improve my understanding. However, in the end, it's led to healthier relationships with the professionals I count on. Eventually, through improved knowledge, communication, and self-reliance, I don't need to ask the same questions any more.

Your perception matters. You need to know you have the right to expect a complete and accurate understanding of what's happening with your money. If your advisor is not the best resource to help you get there, you may need another advisor, or at least outside information to communicate more effectively. Both you and your advisor need to be patient enough to provide you with the knowledge you need to make confident decisions. Furthermore, if you can't get it, then don't invest until you do.

What happens when the advisor feels strongly that you need to reevaluate your perception because it may be holding you back from making the best decisions? Sandy and Heather, life partners, had this kind of experience with their advisor. Here, Heather shares their story:

Heather: Sandy and I have been together for more than 20 years, but we always kept our investments in two completely separate compartments, "hers" and "hers." We shared expenses, but there was some inequity because one of us had accumulated substantially more assets prior to the relationship. Over time, we had developed a totally segregated way of thinking about our assets. However, we did not realize this perspective was preventing us from operating as a "team" with our long-term planning. We had neglected to consider estate tax laws and how each of us would be affected by the loss of the other person. When we met with our new advisor, we were promptly enlightened and saw things clearly for the first time. We had been so glued to our former point of view and the piecemeal system we had previously used for managing our investments. I think we knew subconsciously we were in over our heads, but we were stuck in the habit of our familiar perception. Our new advisor redirected our thinking and taught us new ways to develop strategies. Now we are successfully retired. I am convinced this is largely because we were encouraged to examine and change our perspective and focus on our master plan as a couple.

What can you expect from your advisor as you face so many critical decisions?

You'll want to have reasonable expectations. Your advisor—just like your doctor, accountant, attorney, or any other professional—won't hold your hand through every little decision and give you hours of time just to help you understand what you should know. You may need to take responsibility and find out for yourself. But anyone who expects to help you make important decisions about your life must also understand that you are in charge and your best interests must come first.

Chapter 17

Crises Are Like Little Gifts

Several years ago I had an unexplained pain in my chest on the left side. I instantly thought I was having a heart attack. In a state of panic, I called one of my clients, a cardiologist, and asked to be seen immediately. I was convinced I was in the middle of a health crisis.

I soon learned there was nothing wrong with my heart. I had actually torn my left intercostal muscle, which sits just beneath the heart. I had injured myself lifting weights on the bench press and hadn't recognized it at the time.

During the appointment, my doctor suggested I have some other tests because I have a family history of heart disease. One of the tests included blood work for cholesterol levels. I learned that my LDL cholesterol levels were unusually high. Although I'd been an athlete all my life with excellent eating habits, I'd never focused particularly on lowering my cholesterol. In addition, I had never recognized the potential for genetics to affect me this way.

This experience taught me I needed to pay special attention to exactly what I was eating and how I was managing stress. I had to make some significant changes in my exercise program while more strictly monitoring my food intake. As a result, I dramatically changed my cholesterol levels and created a healthy balance.

What would have happened if I had never torn my intercostal muscle? If the injury hadn't drawn me to the doctor's visit that led to more tests, how would I ever have known there was a potential problem?

Crises are like little gifts. Whether it's a health crisis, like my (thankfully) false alarm, or a financial crisis, like a stock market crash or the loss of a job, every crisis presents opportunities to learn.

Crises Force You to Examine Your Behavior

The investment markets are complex, full of ups and downs and events we cannot predict or control. A financial crisis can feel like an erupting volcano that disrupts our sense of security. Our first impulse is to grab all our money, hold it in our arms, and run briskly to safety, preferably to some dark quiet place where no one can find us.

The panic of the crisis can prompt varying reactions. Some investors have adopted an all or nothing approach. They think that by doing "nothing" with their investments they can avoid a crisis. Other investors assume a crisis will occur no matter what, so why worry about it? Why not just throw something in every direction?

Neither of these approaches is realistic or responsible. It's far more prudent to choose a third response, which is to use the crisis as an incentive to examine your behavior.

First, reevaluate your asset allocation. Did you have too high a percentage of your money in equities (stocks) or other assets that were not easily transferrable to cash (illiquid) or high risk?

Second, of those stocks that you were invested in, did they outperform their respective benchmarks? (These are the guidelines for performance evaluation in various asset classes, such as the S&P 500 Index.) If not, and if they have not had a history of outperformance over a long period of time, you need to reconsider who has your equity money and the strategy you are using.

Third, was your fixed income money truly the "safe" investment that it is supposed to be, or did you take chances with the money that was supposed to be rock solid? Were your bonds appropriately diversified? Did you stick with investment-grade securities, or did you accept lower quality investment choices because you were chasing yield? Did you take the time to understand your investments and analyze the risk levels?

Questions like these help you to appraise your conduct and rethink your strategy going forward. Let's say that in the downturn of 2008 your investments depreciated by 50%. How can you use this experience to begin to recover your assets and be better prepared for the next market downturn?

There's no need to panic in a crisis. The key is in how you manage the crisis and use it to gain a thoughtful perspective of your priorities and behavior. Your first responsibility as an investor is to protect your money and your sense of security. Then you can focus on income and growing your assets. This kind of examination should become a habit because investing is a long-term process. You need these skills in place for many years.

It's Foolish to Waste a Good Crisis

You have to view each crisis as an opportunity to mature as an investor. It's up to you to recognize what each learning experience means to you. No one else can tell you how the crisis has affected you or what lessons you can learn.

Not everyone does this. Some investors have an emotional reaction to the crisis. They get upset, they get frustrated, or they feel a lot of stress, and this range of emotions is the extent of their reaction. But they're wasting the experience; they haven't discovered the learning opportunity.

Study what you could have done differently and decide what you will do differently next time. The answer might be something as simple as realizing, "I should have paid more attention. I didn't want to hear bad news, so I tuned it out." The answer could be, "I was undisciplined with my spending habits, and I didn't really think about the consequences of my actions." The learning could be very simple, but the point is that when a crisis occurs and everything explodes, you have to force yourself to look honestly at what's happened. Each crisis brings with it an entirely new set of learning experiences that can be embraced and used to strategize for the next series of crises, which are sure to lie ahead.

Crises Give You a Chance to Gain Objectivity

One benefit of a crisis is it gives you the chance to gain objectivity. Often, that level of objectivity is missing from the investor's mindset. In good times investors become emotionally involved with their investments. When markets decline, they can even become more committed to the item that hurts them the most. In a crisis, you take on a new perspective. Enlightened, you can look at your investments with fresh eyes, facing facts and examining choices, risks, and results.

One way of doing this is to assign your own grading system to your investments. For example, an "A" investment is 100% reliable in the long term, even if its current market value, in your mind, is temporarily down. This investment may have official "backing" such as a U.S Government security or AAA-insured municipal bond. A "B" investment is one that may seem sound, but for whatever reason you are questioning it at the moment. These are investments to reevaluate in 3 to 6 months. A "C" investment is one that appears to be a mistake. With your C investments, you have to stop being delusional. It's possible that selling them, taking your losses, and reinvesting elsewhere may be the best choice.

After you grade your investments, you need to strictly reevaluate what you own. For each investment, ask yourself if it is something that has the capacity to recover and if waiting is your best option. Or is it an investment that is best replaced because another alternative might perform better in less time? These decisions are best made in conjunction with an advisor, and they should be contemplated with a high level of detail.

But what if you find yourself in the middle of a crisis, and there is no advisor? That is what happened to Miles and Alicia. Miles is a successful dentist with a thriving practice. Over the years, he and Alicia saved and invested diligently, making their decisions independently by reading and studying the markets. As the markets became more volatile and unpredictable, Miles found himself distracted from the priorities of running his practice. To improve his focus, he delegated this responsibility back to Alicia, who felt under-qualified to handle the task. This strained their relationship and did not resolve their investment needs. They realized they had to use this crisis to reevaluate their investments, and that began with getting professional objectivity.

Miles: We thought we could handle everything—my work, the kids, our money, you name it. After all, we were educated, conservative, and committed to what was best for our family.

Alicia: Things that seemed small just got bigger and bigger until we couldn't tell the difference between what was important and what was not. It seems absurd, looking back now, but it's as if we were muddled in our own confusion. We were second-guessing ourselves. We were paralyzed, and we didn't know where to turn.

Miles: At this point, I became worried about our future security. Handling our investments became so complicated that it was detracting from my professional life. It wasn't fair to expect Alicia to step up and take care of things without the right support and guidance. We realized it was time to get a professional's help before it got even more complicated. Our friends helped us to locate an advisor who was sympathetic and highly competent.

Alicia: The fact is, if we hadn't experienced the difficult investment environment, we may never have realized how much we needed to make this change. In a way, I am so grateful we learned this lesson before it was too late.

Crises Give You an Opportunity to Enhance Communication with the Important Players

When you develop an investment strategy and you feel optimistic about its potential, it can be challenging to consider or discuss what can go wrong. People don't like to talk about what could actually go wrong with an investment strategy and where that could leave them. However, this kind of analysis is critical to the process. By working through multiple "what if" scenarios, you can understand the potential financial impact of a crisis before it occurs.

The turmoil gives you an opportunity to communicate more thoroughly with people who may be in an appropriate position to help you, such as your financial advisor. This kind of collaborative dialogue may refine your skills at what I call "x-ray emotional access." A sensitive and thoughtful advisor should imagine how you would feel about an investment decision. Likewise, you should step into the mind of the advisor and contemplate the advisor's logic for the recommendations. The more "x-ray accessibility" an advisor and investor have into each other, the better they can anticipate each other's reactions. The advisor anticipates what the client needs, and the investor can interpret and understand the advisor's advice. This exchange strengthens their relationship and their decision-making strategies.

Ideally, the advisor and client emerge from each crisis better informed and with a revitalized approach to handling investments the next time around.

Crises Force You to Reevaluate Your Priorities

The most important concept to remember—and this is the hardest one of all—is that if the crises never came, we would never be forced to reevaluate our way of doing things. Then one day, the mother of all crises would arrive, and we would be ill-equipped to survive it because we wouldn't have taken advantage of the learning along the way.

Perhaps the best example of this can be illustrated in my recent discussion with Alex.

Saly: You have been successful in diverse businesses over a long period of time. Recently you went through a period where you experienced a very serious illness. What were you like before, and how has this health crisis changed you?

Alex: As far as business, I think I learned that it's not as important as you think. When you get a call and hear the *cancer* word, frankly, you don't care about anything trivial. This all goes out the window. You quickly learn whether you have developed a reliable, independent organization. If you are not there, can the business function, and will its ultimate mission be achieved? Even though you don't plan on it, this becomes a litmus test for your ultimate goal, which is to train your replacement. As long as you are in a state of mind that you are strong and healthy, you may not deal with these issues, and it's easy to put them off. A health crisis can change your thinking and help you to mature as a leader and a builder, versus being a practitioner. Surround yourself with good people, invest in their growth, give them authority, and they'll rise to the top. Learn to get that rookie off the bench and give that person a shot. Turn adversity into opportunity.

Saly: What about your relationships with other people, particularly relative to your tolerance? Are you more selective in your choices?

Alex: I wouldn't wish my cancer on anybody, but I was politely told to "get my affairs in order." When it happened, I reflected on my life and imagined what others would say about how I have lived and what I have done. You very quickly assess what your priorities have been and maybe filter through what you truly wish they were. And yes, having been through all this, it has affected my relationships. One thing I learned is that it is all about relationships. It's not about net worth, or how late I stayed, or the next deal. When you go through a serious illness, there's a tension of what I call "the moment." Until this situation arrives, you're not forced to think about it. When you find yourself in that "moment," you say, "I should pull off to the side of the road and smell the roses because that would be a good thing to do right now." On the other hand, you say, "I want to be significant, and I want to spend my 'moments' on things that are going to continue. Therefore, I need to focus and live my life as if I am going to live another 30 years, and not spend my whole day walking around smelling roses and getting nothing done." Every day I question, "Should I be sitting right here, doing just this; and how many more 'moments' do I have?" Ultimately, of course, we all deal with these things, but when suddenly the time comes and you are forced to think about it, you do. And after you hear the magic words, "I think you're going to be okay now," there is a natural tendency to drift back into the opium of chaos or insignificant activity. I believe we are meant to be human "beings" and not human "doings," and sometimes we put too much emphasis on "doing" instead of just "being."

Saly: There is an argument to be made that through "better being" comes "better doing," but more "doing" doesn't necessarily lead to better "doing."

Alex: Bob Buford's book, *Halftime,* has sharpened my views. I can summarize the first half of my life as "substance." You work hard and acquire assets. I think the second half should be about "significance." Do things that are truly worthwhile, enhancing, and empowering to other people. But again, I go back to balance. I think all of us should strive to achieve balance in everything. This is where the financial advisor can be a great resource. This is a person you're ultimately going to trust; someone who has a demonstrative balance and strong sense of objectivity and support.

Alex used his health crisis as a significant opportunity to reevaluate his entire life. While he battled back for his health, he gained much more as he capitalized on spending time with his family, letting his employees show what they can do, and improving relationships that were important to him.

When you find yourself in a crisis, you have the opportunity to critically examine yourself and rebalance your life. But you don't have to literally experience a crisis of such magnitude to get the value of its teachings. Instead, you can use the concept of a crisis to shift your perspective. One exercise I recommend is to consider your *financial obituary.*

It's About More Than the Money

A financial obituary is the sum total of the achievements your investments will have earned at the end of your life. Imagine next to your actual tombstone a financial tombstone describing the way you managed your money. What would it say? Would it say, "He saved every penny and lived with frugality?" Would it say, "She spent wildly, irresponsibly, and never had anything left?"

What would you want your financial obituary to say about you? You might want it to say you were thoughtful, practical, and well balanced. Perhaps it would say that you didn't "nickel and dime" people but rather held that, financially, things would ultimately even out in the long run. It might say that although you knew money was important, you weren't compulsive about it. Perhaps you were extraordinarily generous to a number of charitable organizations and individuals in need. Maybe you examined your priorities carefully, made thoughtful decisions, didn't act impulsively, and yet once in a while you knew how to have some fun.

What would be on your financial obituary? When you have a sense of what you'd like your financial obituary to say, you can look at your life and ask yourself, "Is that how I am actually living? Is my behavior truly demonstrative of my ultimate financial vision?"

In a recent conversation with Alex, he reminded me of an Amish saying: "We grow too early old, too late smart." When you see each crisis as a little gift, you can absorb some of the wisdom to improve your life, personally and financially.

Chapter 18

The Most Valuable Things in Life Do Not Involve Currency

Young child: What makes a person really wealthy?

Wise elder: You are truly wealthy when you are satisfied with what you have.

When you reflect on what you truly value in your life, does it come down to money? If you had an hour to live, how would you describe the extraordinary moments of your life? Perhaps you would talk about some of your accomplishments, experiences, and people who have meant the most to you. Maybe you would express some regrets and share some great stories. But would you focus on the money? What do you think?

Money is only a part of everything that's important in your life. More money isn't going to get you a rich and meaningful relationship. On the other hand, the reverse may be true. Focusing on improving a relationship may make you happier and consequently more productive—which can lead to an economic benefit.

It's a reflection of our culture and our values that we are so easily consumed by thoughts of money and hopes of where it can lead us. We've become so addicted to short-term results that we will do anything to get them. Sometimes we even compromise our long-term vision to get what we want immediately. Have you ever done this? Certainly we all have to one degree or another. However, when we become hyper-focused on money and insistent on instant results, we end up selling ourselves short.

Money, although central and essential, is not paramount. As we continue to discuss your financial future, we need to maintain a perspective on the whole picture of your life. You have to keep both your happiness and the money in mind. Recognize that these two factors are not the same. Sometimes we forget this and become focused on the money to the exclusion of everything else. Let's examine a few examples of investors who have wrestled with these issues.

Paula and Maureen

Paula and Maureen are sisters in their 50s, with very different personalities and value systems. Their mother, divorced and now deceased, was an extremely affluent woman. However, she was not receptive to any family discussion about estate planning techniques or the dissemination of her assets. Unfortunately, as she aged, she struggled with dementia and depression. By default, Paula became the designated caretaker, as she lived in the home with her mother where she had been raised. Maureen was occupied with her career and her own family and stayed to the sidelines, assuming Paula was agreeable to this responsibility.

When their mother died, she left a substantially higher percentage of her assets to Paula. There was no explanation of the reasoning for this in their mother's will. Paula felt guilty, and Maureen felt hurt and betrayed. The sisters bickered during the next 2 years of the estate distribution. Each one blamed the other for the inequity of the asset distribution. The issues remained unresolved, and their seemingly solid relationship deteriorated. To this day, they remain estranged.

Ironically, despite the unequal division, their mother's estate distribution left both Paula and Maureen with more money than they could ever possibly spend. Clearly the rift in the relationship wasn't just about the money. What was it about? Was it about their mother loving one sister more, or perhaps "repaying" that sister back for her care? Was it about the mother's loss of cognitive function late in life, and no collaborative effort by her and her daughters to address it in her legal documents? Was it about poor communication? Paula and Maureen did not want to take up these issues during the estate distribution because they were so focused on the inheritance. In the end, each sister inherited substantial wealth and paid the price of losing not only their mother but also their relationship with each other.

Many lessons can be learned from this sad story. Previous chapters of this book may come to mind for you. The "fire" broke out without their mother having held a preemptive "drill" (Chapter 7, "The Time to Have the Fire Drill Is Not in the Middle of the Fire"), nor had she planned what she wanted to accomplish (Chapter 10, "Know What You Want to Accomplish"). Perhaps if Paula and Maureen's mother had engaged in professional planning in advance, she could have saved her daughters the bewilderment and distress of a permanently lost relationship.

Elliott

Elliott and Sheryl's father was a widower in the cardboard packaging business. From the time they were teenagers, both Elliott and Sheryl helped in the company and later were promoted to management positions. With their involvement, the business became even more successful. Eventually, as their father expressed interest in retiring, Elliott took on a greater role, making the company the focus of his career. Sheryl's goals were different; she always wanted to pursue a career as an elementary schoolteacher. That dream could not be realized while she was a parent of four children and absorbed in the family business. Elliott and Sheryl agreed that the business, while ideal for Elliott, was not the best place for Sheryl.

Even while absent, their father remained a controlling influence. Twenty years later, when the business received a purchase offer, he was strongly in favor of the transaction. At his direction, the proceeds of the sale were placed in a trust that dramatically benefited Sheryl more than Elliott.

When Elliott and Sheryl's father made this decision, he reasoned that Sheryl hadn't been as involved in the business over the years and therefore hadn't benefited from the business as Elliott had. Elliott, after all, had been getting an income from the business for many years and had participated in the company's success in various ways.

Sheryl never knew about the details of the distribution, especially the inequity, but Elliott did because he handled the logistics of the transaction. Elliott was named as a trustee for Sheryl's trust and felt the pressure of a conflict of interest. He was deeply hurt, and he became embittered over his perception of the discrimination that had occurred. As time went on, the rift in the family, once a small crack, became a large crater. Elliott was increasingly uncomfortable around his sister. He was angry and resentful toward his father, whom he thought had treated him unfairly. Their father was irritated by Elliott's reaction. He thought he was doing the right thing by giving Sheryl more money and evening out his children's participation in the business. Ultimately, every relationship in the family suffered as a result of this one financial decision. Years went by and these issues remained unaddressed and unresolved.

Fifteen years later, Elliott, at the height of his frustration and despair, hired a financial advisor to help him manage his personal assets and the assets of the trust, where he had been reluctantly serving as a trustee. The advisor soon recognized the distribution of the trust assets had led to dissent and disharmony among the family members. This discord had even spread to the next generation, including Elliott and Sheryl's children. The advisor counseled Elliott that the family investment strategy, which included Sheryl, could not be properly formed without consideration of all the parties. Additionally, this process might include a possible redesign of the asset distribution.

The advisor traveled to speak face to face with Elliott and Sheryl's father. Here is what the advisor said to him: "We are not well acquainted, and I hope you can appreciate my respectful intentions. Your family is dividing, and I implore you to work with me to find a fair resolution to these painful circumstances. Although you are in your late 80s, you still have the power to meet everyone's needs, including your own, and repair the rift that has wounded the people you love. We can fix this; I know it. I will stay with you, committed to the task, until we find something sensible that works for everyone. Surely in your last moments of life you do not want to remember that you could have done something about this and you lacked the courage to find a better solution for everyone."

What happened next changed the lives of 16 people. The advisor helped the father to reorganize his personal assets, permitting more money than he had previously thought was available to transition to Elliott, thereby rebalancing the inequity. This was a tremendous relief to Elliott, who could manage his own retirement and help his four children. The emotional lift to Elliott was equally important. Elliott had waited a long time for his father's approval and appreciation of his accomplishments in the business.

The advisor suggested that Sheryl should be properly informed of the new financial strategy. Therefore, she could become more educated about her own financial responsibilities. Sheryl's needs were satisfied by a change in the trustee arrangement, which included open communication and access to investment assets. This put her in a better position to offer assistance to her three children, two of whom had newborns. Through all these changes, their father's income was not compromised, and he could maintain his quality of life. Elliott and

Sheryl reconciled, renewing relationships with each other's children, their father, and each other. To this day, that same advisor works successfully with all these family members.

What these stories illustrate is how deeply divided people can become over money—even when there's plenty of it to go around. In Paula and Maureen's case, their relationship became defined negatively by the division of assets. In Elliott and Sheryl's case, the rifts were healed. But in both cases, the resentment caused by money stole valuable time from generations of family relationships. How much better might it have been for these investors to enjoy both the money *and* the relationships with their families?

Compare these stories now to another investor who recently was reminiscing about his financial and family life while growing up.

Tom

Tom, now a successful executive, grew up in a lower-middle-class urban neighborhood. His family had minimal resources and few material possessions of value. He shares his favorite childhood memory of the time he spent with his father every evening when he returned home from work. "My dad was home every night at 6 p.m., and before dinner he would throw a ball around with me in the yard. Every night, my dad was there, ready to play. Sometimes other kids from our neighborhood would come over and hang out with us. Despite the fact that we had so little, it never occurred to me that we didn't have anything. I didn't know the difference. I felt like a million bucks at the end of each day because I had my dad with me."

What are you doing when you come home after a tough day? Are you throwing the ball around with your kids or someone you care about? If you're so busy making money that you're not receiving this message, then you're spending another kind of currency.

Helping investors with their money for so many years, I've had the opportunity to observe people through their lives as they've grown up and had children. Many of those children have had children. What do people value above all? Even though I'm in the money business, I recognize that money is not what people hold in highest regard at the end of the day.

The most valuable things in life do not involve currency. You need money to purchase certain things such as food and shelter and vehicles, but if you focus completely on the money, you'll miss the other experiences that are important to you—those that you are using the money to get to! How are you spending your life on a day-to-day basis? Are you giving up what you say you want to make the money to get what you already have?

If you become too fixated on the money, you can miss too much of what's most important. You need balance. If you're settling for an advisor who isn't interested in the rest of your life, then you are aiming too low. Your advisor is a facilitator who can help manage not only your investment strategy, but also the monetary dynamics of your family.

At the same time, you and your advisor need to recognize that a financial advisor still has a job to do, and that can't be denied. The love and attention advisors offer is admirable, but if they don't know how to direct clients in handling money, they are not fulfilling their responsibility as professionals. Investing *is* about the money, and it's also about a lot of other attributes, such as caring, educating, advocating, comforting, communicating, strategizing, and many other factors that contribute to a healthy, collaborative relationship. It is the combination of all these attributes that make the relationship complete. Remember, no relationship is perfect. We're all human. But by keeping financial decisions in the context of your entire life and approaching money from that broad perspective, the advisor keeps you centered on what is most valuable to YOU.

Leo is an investor who genuinely appreciates the value of his life. Now in his 90s, he reflects on his successes and failures with a thoughtful point of view. Here he shares his wisdom.

Leo: When I was young, I was a daily drinker. I was drunk every day for 10 years. I had my last automobile accident the Friday before Thanksgiving. I knew I was in trouble, but I didn't want to go to AA. I thought I could do it myself. I would get up every morning and say, "This is it. I am never going to drink again." By night I was drunk again. Finally, my wife Peggy got me into AA. There I learned the only requirement for membership is the desire to stop drinking. In my first meeting I heard that, and I said, "That's me. This is going to work." And I haven't picked up a drink since. I went to a meeting every day; I went to meetings wherever I was. I have been sober for 40 years, and I still go to four meetings a week.

Saly: What was the connection in finding sobriety and developing the idea for your business, which led to financial prosperity?

Leo: I thought of the idea for our business while I was still drinking, but I wasn't able to do anything about it. When I got into AA, I got sober, and my life changed. My mind cleared, my enthusiasm increased, and my health improved. Then I said to myself, "Now I can get into this."

Saly: When you look back at what you have accomplished in both your business and in life, what advice would you give to a young person just getting started?

Leo: The first thing I would say is whatever career you enter, work hard. That was the biggest part of my success.

Saly: Now you have achieved both affluence and influence. You have considerable wealth and a strong philanthropic drive. You are blessed with your family around you. What is most important to you right now?

Leo: My values. My eight kids. My current wife, Betty, whom I was lucky to meet later in life. My first wife Peggy (now deceased) and I were married 60 years, and she went through hell with me while I was drinking. When the company went public, we merged all the stock, and I ended up getting 5% of the company. Everyone else in the family got more than me.

Saly: Do you have any regrets about that?

Leo: No. Originally when I set up the company, we were really small. I gifted stock to everybody. I thought if we were successful, they will all own stock, and I won't have to go through gifting the money to them in the end. And now I don't have to leave anything to my children. Now I can use all my money, and they are all millionaires. One of my sons lives in a $5 million house on the ocean. I live here in a $325,000 house that we love. Betty and I are both really happy.

Saly: What makes you angry now?

Leo: Absolutely nothing. I don't get angry about anything. If anything gets me worked up, I just walk away. It's not worth it. I've made a decision in my life to forgive and not hold on to anger.

Saly: I've heard you say you're a simple man. You certainly have enough money to have whatever you desire. What could you possibly wish for?

Leo: With each new day, I wish to be grateful for everything I have, and everything I have had.

Clearly all that Leo has learned and accomplished is about so much more than the money.

Chapter 19

Find the Courage You Need to Have Integrity

Throughout this book we have talked at length about responsibility. We've discussed that even though it may be hard to admit, most of us have either participated in or benefited from a boom that eventually led to an economic downturn. An integral part of the healing process is acknowledging your part in events that went the wrong way. By taking responsibility for your role in your financial circumstances, you can position yourself to improve them.

But it doesn't stop there. As you move forward armed with new ideas and improved strategies for investing, you need to be prepared to follow through on your commitments to yourself. In addition to taking responsibility, you also need to have integrity. Values do not necessarily develop as a result of being successful, yet you can become very successful as a result of developing values. Your values and clear sense of integrity must come first.

In investing, there's no guarantee you won't hit another financial crisis. In fact, it's more likely to happen than not. Even if you're taking responsibility for your money, things can still go awry. We could make the argument that the situation has nothing to do with you—that you are a victim of what's happening, and you have to just accept what comes to you. However, there's still no excuse for not making an effort to contribute to a constructive solution, even if that solution only applies to how you're going to handle things. Having integrity involves recognizing not just what role you have already played, but also what role you could play. Integrity means having the courage to accept responsibility and stand behind your convictions.

Think for a moment about victims of a random catastrophe—perhaps a devastating earthquake or a serious car crash. Even if the people involved are truly injured parties—innocent bystanders suddenly harmed by an unforeseen event—they still have a choice as to how they respond. They can either become victims and remain in the rubble, or they can rise up and become part of the solution. They may be justified in feeling that the situation is not at all their fault. That does not mean that it's healthy for them to do nothing.

If you happened to be near the site of a hypothetical "earthquake," would you continue to stand immobile? You didn't bring the earthquake on, and it's not even your job to help clean up the mess, but would you idly watch people crawling out from among all the rocks? Or would you pull yourself out and then help others? You have the same choice when it comes to your money. If you want to survive and live a happy and prosperous life, you need to have the courage and integrity to pull yourself out of your current situation and become part of the solution.

To have integrity in your financial choices means constantly evaluating yourself. Ask yourself daily, "How am I doing? Am I living in accordance with my priorities? Am I following through on my master plan?" The choices we make each and every day are the ones that create the results we realize in the long run. Regardless of what the market has done or how disappointed you may be in others, or whether they have done the job you pay them to do, the question you need to ask is, "What have *I* done today to contribute to the situation *I'm* in?" Ask yourself at the end of every day, "How have I lived up to my potential today?"

Try this exercise. Before you go to bed tonight, give yourself a report card for the day. Evaluate yourself across a number of dimensions.

- In my job today, how well did I perform? Was I responsive and supportive of my coworkers? Did I hear what they had to say, or did I interrupt them because I was pursuing my own agenda? Did I use my power unfairly in any way?

- In my family, was I kind and understanding? Did I look beyond verbal dialogue and consider my loved ones' body language? Did their communication coincide well with what they had to say? Was I short-tempered, and did I lose my patience?

- In my health and fitness, did I eat in accordance with my long-term health goals? Did I exercise vigorously and challenge myself to improve my overall fitness?

- In my character, was I an inspiration to others, or did I drag people down? Did I look for ways, such as with sense of humor, to improve the mood of others?

- In my life, was I thinking about the global picture, or was I caught up in materialistic distractions or meaningless minutiae?

The answers to these questions, and others, go into your personal grade for the day. Every category may not get the same grade. Maybe you gave yourself an A in business, but you gave yourself a C in family relations.

It's challenging to complete this evaluative process and grade yourself every day. You might be thinking, "Can't I limit this to once a week?" But emotional shortcuts are the opposite of integrity. It's the DAILY process of evaluation that makes the exercise so powerful. As soon as you get away from daily evaluation, you lose track of the specifics. After a few days, all the events of the past week start to blur together. It's difficult to remember the decisions you made, the actions you took, and the consequences they had. Or worse, as the days pass, it's easy to rationalize them away. Time makes it easier for you to be less than honorable in your assessment of what took place. Maybe you've now found a way to justify your actions. That remark you made that hurt someone's feelings 3 days ago? You can lay the blame on someone else—after all, that person made you mad and prompted you to say it. Maybe you ate poorly or missed a critical appointment, but you can excuse yourself because you were so hungry at the time or were stuck in traffic. Our first inclination when we make a mistake is to defend ourselves. Our mechanism for developing excuses is so well refined it's as though we have the excuses ready, just in case we need them! As with other issues we've discussed earlier, if we permit excuses and rationalizations to proliferate, all we do is suspend a fair evaluative process and delay self-improvement. If you want to act with integrity, you must have the courage to be honest in your assessment. You need to do this now and make it a lifelong habit.

Let's explore for a minute a related habit, one you may want to minimize or eliminate: use of the word "try." What do people mean when they say they "try" to do something? It means they are stating their intention and not promising anything further. It's as if they think they deserve "credit" for their intention! Sometimes you will even hear the overt plea, "At least give me credit for trying."

Here is an example: "I 'tried' to call you." What does this mean? Does it mean your house flooded in the middle of dialing and you had to run outside? Did you break your finger while dialing? Did you get interrupted by something more pressing? Would you now like help rationalizing why you never actually went further than intending to call?

The idea of getting "credit" for your intentions is meaningless. That is how we have come to use expressions such as "talk is cheap," or "actions speak louder than words." It's the *doing* that has meaning. It is when your value system and your actions are aligned that you show you have the courage to act with integrity. After all, "tryers" try, and "doers" do.

Consider, for example, a person who is "trying" to quit smoking. The thought process may look something like this:

1. I know I should quit smoking.
2. I choose to quit smoking.
3. I will quit smoking,
4. I have quit smoking.
5. I will never smoke again.
6. I will not be in a room with people who are smoking.
7. I will not associate with someone who smokes.
8. I am committed to helping others quit smoking.

Sometimes we lose our way when the time comes to shift from intentions to actions. This is where we must rely on our integrity. There is no such thing as "trying" to quit smoking. You either smoke, or you don't. As difficult as breaking the habit of smoking may be, removing the word "trying" from your language may be even more difficult! See how many times a day you use the word "try," and ask yourself if you want "credit" for *thinking* instead of *doing*.

There are times when "trying" is an appropriate expression. You may be working diligently at something truly beyond your current capabilities, or you may be in the process of converting intention to action. You may be initiating a change in your behavior, while unsure about which road to take. This is where you have to stop and consider the extent of your commitment and the plan you will follow. When you have the courage of your conviction, you will act, and there will be no more "trying."

Alison has an interesting perspective on recognizing what is in your power and moving from intention to action:

Alison: The recent financial crisis was very rough for my family. My husband, a mid-level manager, was laid off in early 2008, and I was working various part-time jobs to keep us financially afloat. Helplessly, we were waiting for things to change, and of course my husband was anxious to get back into the work stream. It was pretty demoralizing for all of us, and we had to make some major life adjustments. Our advisor reminded us our restricted economics had a silver lining—an opportunity to bond as a family and save money by spending more time together in "free" activities. One day when we were playing Scrabble (a game we could still afford!), my teenage kids suggested we use only words that represented empowerment and achievement. We needed a thesaurus because these words were far from our thinking at the time. This exercise gave us a fresh perspective, and we realized how much we had been pulling each other down. As a family, we resolved to end each day with a new "power word" we could share with one another. Each one of us was responsible for expressing how we could "act out" this word in our behavior each day. We decided to think only in "I" terms, asking ourselves what we could each do to change things on our own. We agreed to obliterate the word "try" from our language, as well as the Scrabble board. This was really difficult. We had fallen into the habit of blaming others, making excuses, and feeling sorry for ourselves. This experience brought us back to life as we changed our attitudes and actions. Shortly after the "Scrabble epiphany," everything started to turn around for us. Was it a coincidence? We'll never know, but we are truly grateful. As a family, we've vowed never to go back to that old way of thinking or speaking.

Alison's story is inspiring, and it's uplifting to see how her children participated in the self-evaluative process. Fortunately, this was followed by a positive outcome. On the other hand, there's a very fine line between beating yourself up and being fair in your assessment of your conduct. It's important that your criticism of yourself be constructive and in the spirit of self-improvement. If you can maintain that supportive outlook, your assessments will be more productive.

Now let's discuss how this applies to your investments. After you accept the responsibility for assessing yourself daily and grading your conduct, you will have some experience with this evaluative process. Next you can translate this behavior into how you handle your investments. Refer back to your life plan as it applies to your finances. As we talked about earlier, this means you must

A. Establish your most important priorities.

B. Rank them.

C. Develop a master plan for your life.

D. Verify that your investments are contributing appropriately toward those goals.

E. Surround yourself with those who are going to support you.

Now honestly evaluate how well you are handling your investments and navigating your life plan.

To be most effective, write down your ranked priorities on a single 3-by-5 card. Make five copies. Post them in areas of your home where you can see them every day, such as on the bathroom mirror, the refrigerator, your calendar, your desk in your office. Look at them often throughout the day and use them to guide your decisions. (Another option is to send a text message to yourself or even a voice mail.) At the end of every day, ask yourself:

- Where have I made mistakes?
- How might I modify my behavior?
- What is within my power to change now?

When you answer these questions, continually keep your priorities in mind. Here are some more specific questions that can help you drill even deeper into the financial aspects of each priority on your list.

Financial security: Did I follow through on my savings goals? Did I communicate clearly with my advisor? Did I ask the questions on my mind, no matter how difficult they were to express? Am I informed, and do I truly understand what's happening with my money? Have I recently reviewed my investment strategy, so it's fresh in my mind? Is my strategy guiding my decisions?

Family: Was I thoughtful and considerate about the entire family's future needs in my spending decisions? Did I contribute to and preserve the money we have set aside for emergencies? Did I contribute to my children's education funds or my own, or my parents' long-term care needs? Am I confident that my will and my trust documents are watertight and up to date? Was I a financially responsible role model for my children today?

Health: Was I honest with myself about how my health affects my financial situation and that of my entire family? How did I improve my health today? Did I invest in my health by exercising, eating well, and taking care of my body? Did I get enough sleep? Am I confident I have the best health insurance, so I can afford whatever medical care my family or I may need?

Career: Did I think about the bottom line (either profits or income) today and how I can improve it? If I am not making the money I want to make, did I find new ways of generating income or growing my investments? If I am satisfied with my income, did I devote sufficient time to maintaining my financial situation? Did I overdo it at the expense of other important priorities? Am I happy in what I'm doing with my career, such that it can contribute to my long-term financial situation?

Hobbies: Are my finances aligned so I can afford my hobbies while honoring my other priorities? Are my hobbies contributing to my overall happiness? Is there any way in which my hobbies are becoming a distraction? Did I pay enough attention to my career and health—recognizing that if I don't, I won't have the means to enjoy my hobbies over the long term?

These tough questions can tempt you to produce a variety of rationalizations and excuses: "The market was terrible. The economy was stagnant. The tax laws changed. The political environment had a negative affect on me. Other people lied to me or misrepresented risk." Here again the familiar habit of deflecting is a challenge that you will have to confront perpetually. This is where courage comes in. Having courage means being true to your goals in spite of what is happening around you.

Taking a principled position on the small but critical issues will eventually play out in the bigger ones. Use the issues of lesser consequences to practice your skills for when you need them most. Don't let your fears paralyze you. Learn to step right up to your doubts, face them head on, and tell yourself, "I am going to take responsibility. I am going to look at what I can do differently. I will act with courage and integrity."

Chapter 20

There's an Entire Economy in What We Consume and Waste

Take a look at the following scenario.

Laura is an investor who has a high-profile career in advertising. Her job involves long hours and an intense work week. She has always focused so completely on the responsibilities of her position that she has rarely found time for herself. Years of a poor diet, lack of exercise, and an accumulation of stress have taken a heavy toll on Laura and her family. As a result, Laura has felt the need for life changes to restore her resilience and enthusiasm.

At the peak of her frustration, Laura made a confession to her financial advisor, someone with experience and interest in health and fitness. She said to the advisor, "Look. I've got these 20 pounds I can't lose. I think I'm depressed. I'm 49 years old. I'm just not feeling right, and I need someone to help me make some changes!" At the recommendation of her advisor, she entered a training program with a fitness professional. Laura's advisor, an experienced athlete, suggested she consider cycling as a way to lose weight, gain fitness, and reduce her stress levels.

Laura carefully researched this and soon bought a bike—a good one. She parked her car in the garage and started to ride. Not too far into the training program she hurt her shoulder lifting weights and had to have reconstructive surgery. This would have been the perfect time for her to say, "Look at that. I dedicated myself to my exercise program, and what did I get? Surgery. Well, this whole fitness thing stinks." But instead she persevered. She rehabilitated herself and got right back into her regimen to lose weight and improve the quality of her life.

Within 2 months, Laura finished a charity cycling event that was 55 miles long. She called her advisor 2 days later. Listen to what she said.

Laura: I must tell you something very personal. Meeting you was the best thing that's ever happened to me, and this goes way beyond investments. I have to explain exactly how you've changed my life.

First of all, I love riding my bike. I'm so happy. When I go out for a ride, I feel all the stress of my day just melt away.

Second, I've always had a great marriage, and I love my husband. But my husband loves to ride his bike outdoors. And because I have a good bike and am now fit enough to ride with him, we are enjoying the kind of time together that we haven't had since we were dating. It has made us closer and our relationship much richer. I don't know how I could have achieved that any other way.

Third, my entire family has changed its behavior. No more pizza. No more French fries. No more soda. We have all reconsidered our eating habits, including how much we consume. We've noticed that it's costing significantly less money to live a healthy lifestyle. Instead of doing sedentary things that can often be expensive, we now find ourselves playing basketball, taking walks, riding our bikes together, and engaging in activities that we've never enjoyed before as a family.

And finally, I'm in the best health of my life. I saw my doctor recently, and together we reviewed my new blood work. I thought there would be some changes, but my doctor was stunned to see the difference. Whereas before I was concerned I might have to go on medication for managing my cholesterol, I no longer have that problem. By modifying the way I eat, exercise, and manage my stress, my body has responded in a way that could lower my health-care concerns and costs for many years into the future.

When you read Laura's story, think about the number of amazing benefits she received just from making the decision to change her eating and exercise habits. What did she improve? Her health, her emotions, her stress level, her relationships, her family life, her cholesterol levels, and maybe even her future need for health care. The way she is living now is a result of that one decision to start riding a bike—a dramatic improvement in her overall life.

So how is Laura's story relevant to a book whose central focus is on managing and investing money? Think about the financial impact of her decision. She drives less, so she pays less for gas. Her car gets less usage, so she pays less in maintenance. Her health is better, so she pays less in medical care. Her stress is down, so she spends less on her old habits like overeating and alcohol. Aside from the personal and emotional benefits of her decision, can you see the economic impact on her life?

Now take it one step further. Laura's decision reaches beyond her own life. It actually affects the world around her. When Laura drives less, she generates less pollution into the air. When her health costs go down, everyone's health costs go down because she becomes one less person likely to need benefits later. Laura also serves as a role model for others, so rather than having just one person making changes that affect the economy, we now have the potential for several.

What if you don't have the time, finances, or inclination to pursue a sport with the same enthusiasm as Laura? You can consider simple changes in your habits that can offer great benefits and influence you in other ways. Here is an example we can all relate to—breakfast! Do you grab something sugary and unhealthy at the last minute because you ran out of time or forgot to eat earlier? A small adjustment in your routine can lead to a great breakfast experience—try oatmeal! Now you have

1. An excellent nutritional start to your day
2. A ritual that gives you a thoughtful moment to yourself
3. A natural way to lower your LDL cholesterol
4. A sense of satiety that will last for much longer than most breakfast alternatives
5. A chance to spend time with other family members as you enjoy table time together
6. A heightened awareness of how healthy eating can contribute to your energy levels
7. A positive example for others who are considering healthy lifestyle changes

Fuel your engine with what it needs to perform. It doesn't have to be complicated. This same logic applies to exercise. Walk as much as you can, for fitness, circulation, relaxation, and meditation. Nature equipped us very well, but we must use what we were given to actually get the benefits—economic and otherwise. Finally, don't underestimate the intrinsic psychological value of truly taking care of yourself!

Although this book is about managing and investing money, I want to pursue a few other relevant thoughts that may strike you at first as more philosophical than financial. Follow along and consider how these subsequent observations could have an enormous impact on the amount of shared wealth and on all our financial futures. In short, an entire economy exists in what we consume and waste.

Think about your garbage. What do you throw out? What do you recycle? How much personal money do you waste, and how much money is spent via taxes to haul it all away? How much waste could you prevent if you composted what can be regenerated and committed yourself to "precycling" (changing your buying habits to avoid products whose packaging does not break down easily)? The day is coming when you will be charged for garbage based on a predetermined volume, and you may not have a choice.

Think about your water usage. How much water do you use when you shower, shave, brush your teeth, or do your laundry? How much money could you save on your water bill if you cut back? How much money would go back into the economy if we as a society worried less about water rights and availability because there would simply be more water available?

Consider how food is wasted. Many restaurants serve a portion size that could feed four! What's the result? You've spent more than you have to, and your weight goes up from overeating. Or you go home with the extra food in a Styrofoam container with plastic silverware in a plastic bag, all of which creates more garbage—along with the leftovers you forget to eat. What if you ordered only what you could finish, or split a meal with someone else? You would be saving money for yourself and for the economy as a whole while improving your health and cutting back on waste.

Now consider what might be the greatest "financial-drain-through-waste" that we suffer as individuals and as a society: health-care needs and costs. What are the economic consequences of our "unhealthiness?" How well do our lifestyle choices tie into our decisions about the growth and maintenance of our investment capital?

There is currently a great deal of attention focused on national health-care reform, but where in the legislation is the part about what WE as individuals have to do? Recently, a forum on National Public Radio predicted that by 2030, health-care costs will amount to 30% of the gross domestic product in the United States. When are we going to ask what responsibility WE have and what actions WE will take to help solve this crisis?

Experience substantiates that people across a variety of circumstances can be spurred into action by being penalized for undesirable behavior and paid for desirable behavior.

Exhibit A: In 2003 in London, UK, the mayor instituted a toll, also known as a "congestion tax," for driving during business hours in a 16-square-mile section of the city (*Forbes*, Oct 5, 2009, p. 38). Congestion and pollution went down significantly, and the use of public transportation increased. Those who drove into the center were "penalized" ($224 million in revenue for the city!), whereas residents and visitors were "paid" with cleaner air and more pleasant conditions. Singapore and Stockholm have similar programs, but we haven't gotten past the proposal stage here in the United States. What are we waiting for?

Exhibit B: During the 2008–2009 school year, in a Philadelphia suburb, Cheltenham High School personnel created an incentive program to improve scores on the Pennsylvania state assessment test (PSSA). Administrators and faculty met with and surveyed 11th grade students to identify appealing incentives. Besides providing motivational speeches and posters, they printed inspirational slogans on pencils to be used for the exam, served breakfast to students on the morning of the exam, and dismissed students from school for the day after the exam. Most important, they promised that if PSSA results met national standards for AYP (Adequate Yearly Progress), students would be treated to a senior trip and would be excused from final exams as seniors—and students failing to show proficiency on the reading or math portions of the PSSA would be mandated to take corresponding remedial courses. When goals were reached, students were assembled for the announcement of a senior trip and cancelation of exams. Then they marched behind the drum corp to the cafeteria for an ice cream social. The enormous enthusiasm and spirit of the students showed the power of incentives.

Exhibit C: On Sept 22, 2009, *The Wall Street Journal* reported research findings that "smoke-free laws reduced the rate of heart attacks by an average of 17% after one year in communities where the bans had been adopted." This is impressive, but there is more! The benefit has been shown to grow with time, and after 3 years the reduction was 26%! A quote in the middle of the article reads, "We turned the ban on, and we watched the heart-attack rate go down." Smokers were "penalized" by being denied the right to smoke, whereas smokers and nonsmokers alike were "paid" with lower health risks.

As a culture, we invest great sums of money in solving problems after they've occurred. How much better off would we all be if we took the personal actions needed to prevent these problems in the first place? Some say that the growing personal savings rate conflicts with our goal of an ascending economy. You may even have heard the refrain, "We have to get the consumer back to borrowing and spending." But is consumption the best stimulant for the economy in the long run? There are entire economies we can bring to the forefront, such as the expansion of nontraditional energy sources, the diminishment of waste, and the prevention of serious health conditions, such as diabetes. These new economies can be funded by the savings generated by our life-style changes. If we stopped wasting so much, we could save, improve our health and that of the earth, and even have room for new consumption, if that is what we truly want.

Let's take a closer look at the economics of a paradigm shift regarding health care. The numbers in the following story add up to an impressive sum and might offer personal relevance to you.

Todd and Margie are a married couple in their mid-50s. Todd has been in manufacturing and has owned his own business for many years. Through years of saving and investing, they've amassed an estate valued at $15 million. Todd and Margie have two children, and they are seeking an efficient transition of their assets to these heirs.

One of their concerns is the extent to which estate taxes will diminish their assets. After consultation with their attorney and financial advisor, they decide to purchase $7.5 million of survivorship insurance. This insurance pays a death benefit when the second spouse dies. In this case, the policy would be held in an irrevocable life insurance trust, placing it outside of the estate and avoiding inadvertent inflation of the estate's value.

The premium Todd and Margie are likely to pay for this policy is about $70,000 per year. The rate estimate is higher than average because Todd is 50 pounds overweight, with high blood pressure and high cholesterol. Todd is what we call "rated," which means the insurance company is pricing the premium at a higher level to compensate for the greater risk of insuring his life.

Todd acknowledges that the insurance quote is quite expensive, and he is very concerned about the health exam that is part of the application process. He and Margie feel hesitant about paying the annual premiums, especially given that they will not receive a benefit during their lifetimes. The purpose of the insurance is to provide liquidity at death, pay estate taxes, or "replace" the value lost to taxes and therefore preserve assets for their heirs. What can Todd do about these high premiums? He decides that he finally must take responsibility for his overall health. Clearly, this is the impetus he needs. Even though it is financially motivated, he knows he needs to make changes in his lifestyle, lose weight, and make his health a priority.

With the guidance of his physician and the support of a personal trainer, Todd begins a dedicated exercise program. He modifies his diet in conjunction with professional advice and loses over 50 pounds. His blood pressure is dramatically lower, and his doctor even suggests he reduce the medication for this condition. Because Todd made significant changes to his diet and exercise routine, his LDL cholesterol goes down from 200 to the low 100s, a level within normal ranges.

After some time in his new regime, Todd takes the insurance health exam. Now he qualifies as "preferred," a rating that is even better than the norm. The insurance company is offering him credit for his impressive health status. What is the premium now? $59,000 per year. Not only do Todd and Margie save $11,000 this year, but they are saving $11,000 per year for as long as they continue to pay into that policy. Todd is 55 and his life expectancy (which by the way he might have extended) could be 30 additional years. He stands to save perhaps $250,000, maybe more, just by improving his health—and that is without compounding the interest!

In this way, Todd is actually being "paid" to be healthier, and he would have been "taxed" or "penalized" for continuing his unhealthy lifestyle. In addition to the many remarkable benefits of becoming healthier, Todd is supported by an incentive structure that motivates him to make the change. As a result of this careful planning, Todd and Margie's children will inherit a more sizable estate.

Now that Todd and Margie have protected their estate, we might look ahead to the future of the wealth they have preserved. How well are their children prepared for this transition and for the ensuing responsibility of managing this vast wealth?

Currently about 78 million U.S. baby boomers are facing retirement. It would seem obvious that this population, with all their education, wealth, and experience, would be inclined to plan well for their futures and those of their children. Is that true? Are we and our children more or less prepared for the challenges ahead?

As a parent of two teenagers, I think about what my children will inherit. It seems to me that we need to examine how we will transfer responsibility, financial and otherwise, to the next generation as they grow into and through adulthood. Just as our human capital generates our financial capital, our children's human capital will be required to maintain and expand the financial capital we pass on to them. This includes the larger issues of consumption, waste, health care, and environmental responsibility.

Do not delude yourself into believing your children will succeed in these responsibilities if you leave them to their own resources. Think about the roots of your own accomplishments. Have your work ethic and your achievements emerged out of a vacuum, or can you trace them to lessons learned from your parents and other influential adults in your young life? Your children need a high level of training if they are to be prepared to respect, honor, preserve, and build on the assets you leave them. Insist that your children assume character-developing and skill-building responsibilities—community service on a regular basis; mentoring of younger children; earning, managing, and saving money. Only then will you have reason to believe that they are well prepared to manage and grow your wealth after you are gone. Only then can you have confidence that what you have accumulated in your lifetime will be a foundation for subsequent future accomplishment.

Plainly and simply, less consumption and less waste equals more money. If you want to have more money, change the way you live. Save and invest that money. Not only will you be helping yourself in many ways, but you will be supporting the planet both financially and environmentally.

True prosperity is about so much more than the money. Each of us has the power to change our behavior, and each of us has a responsibility to our children, to our community, and to the world at large. We are all capable of committing to a lifestyle that supports sustainability and benefits the greater good.

Chapter 21

Make It Happen

Economic downturns can bring an almost unbearable level of pain, hardship, and disappointment for many investors. When there's a crisis or the bursting of a bubble, everyone in the vicinity is affected. It's difficult to accept failure at such a grand level. And it's almost impossible to accept the thought that something so overwhelming and terrible could happen to any of us. Failure hurts. But failure can pay off significantly in learning, growth, and wisdom. We've all made mistakes, and we've paid the price. Now where can we go from here?

When I first started in the brokerage business in 1980, I had just completed my degree in psychology from Cornell University. What could I possibly have known about investments at such a young age and with so little experience? The economy was in bad shape, interest rates were well into the double digits, and inflation was skyrocketing. I could have viewed this as an inauspicious starting point. Fortunately, I had the opposite perspective. After all, things couldn't get much worse, could they? I was determined, right from the start, to make as many mistakes as possible, as early on as possible, to "get them out of the way" as I grew into my career. Little did I realize I would continue to make mistakes long after I intended to get these behind me! We all experience failure at one time or another, and we can't control the timing of its arrival or departure. It's what we do with our experience that matters most. We must use each "failure," no matter how insignificant, to balance our emotions, reexamine our priorities, and adjust our strategy. Failure provides us with the greatest payoff of all—another chance! Now is the time to make the most of that opportunity.

Each of us is responsible to steer our life in the direction we want it to go. Although we can't control others, we can control ourselves and our actions.

To tie together the last 20 chapters, I'd like to leave you with a few summary observations. Collectively, they can help you review the key points of this book.

Respect Rules, but Appreciate Them for What They Are

Rules give intelligent structure to your decisions. They can help you remain true to your mission, limit errors, and provide a template for those who come after you. You need rules for personal conduct relative to your finances: manage your expenses, generate income, grow capital, and establish life priorities. You need specific rules to govern your investment strategies: liquidity, transparency, personal understanding, regulation, and the character of your advisors. You need general rules, otherwise known as investment objectives, to guide the level of risk you are willing to take in exchange for growth opportunities. However, following even the most well-thought-out rules does not guarantee results. It only increases the probabilities.

Choose Your Financial Advisor Deliberately and Carefully

This decision must be the result of extensive research and consideration. Take recommendations from trusted associates. Interview multiple advisors, including people who work with them and invest with them. Don't settle for a financial advisor whose focus is solely on the management of your money. You can do better than that. You deserve a financial advisor who shares your philosophies and is committed to providing you and your investments with the level of care you expect. In addition, this advisor should also be prepared to counterweight your personal biases and help you manage your emotions when it comes to investments. Your advisor should be dedicated to the over-all well being of you and your family. After a careful and deliberate search has put you in league with a qualified financial advisor, monitor your relationship to be confident you are continuing to receive the performance and service that meets your standards and expectations.

Take Responsibility

Only you can decide what your life can be, and neither you nor your financial advisor can make responsible investment moves in the absence of that decision. Rank your priorities, and from that list develop a master plan that will take you from where you are to where you want to be. When you have committed to a strategy, take responsibility for completing the journey. Don't rely on your financial advisor to make decisions that are rightfully yours to make. If you don't understand enough to take responsibility for a decision, keep asking questions until you do. It's your money. If you need the help of a trusted friend to support you along the way, as Jiminy Cricket did for Pinocchio, so be it—or you might serve as your own conscience. However you go about it, be realistic with yourself. Be honest about what you should do, and what you should not do, such as invest with friends, overextend credit, get too attached to something you know you should sell, or live the consequences of someone else's actions. Instead of making excuses after the fact, recognize your tendencies and thinking patterns beforehand and avoid poor choices in advance. No more blaming others, either. This is your life to live! When you take responsibility, you will feel confident and in command, and you'll improve the probability of more favorable outcomes.

Plan

Know what you want to accomplish and develop a long-term strategy. Just as you'll want your tax and estate planning and gifts to others on paper, you'll also want to plan—with your advisor—your asset allocation and investment strategy. In the absence of a plan, you and your heirs are susceptible to facing important decisions in the middle of a crisis. That can lead to choices you later regret, often followed by more compromised thinking and other poor choices. Regardless of what events or crises lie ahead for you, you'll still need a detailed financial plan that takes inflation into account. Use the nine steps from Chapter 12, "Expect to Pay a Price—Either Now or Later—for the Choices You Make About Handling Your Money," to mathematically calculate what actions you need to take to achieve financial independence. Follow the plan and evaluate your progress while keeping your highest priorities in mind. Remember, just because something is available does not mean it is free! Each choice comes with a price, and you're going to pay it sooner or later. Only you can decide when to pay the price.

Be Strong

First, put yourself in a position of strength by working from a base of what you know best. You have acquired skills and knowledge that amount to human capital. Spend that capital wisely. Don't let enthusiasm over making money or the enticement of a particular project lure you into an enterprise where you lack the requisite skills and knowledge. If you do, you risk losing capital and becoming distracted, thus lowering the probability of success in the endeavor where you have the greatest leverage.

Second, make sure your thinking is based on reality. Many investors' financial decisions are weakened by wishful thinking (probably grandmother will leave me a bundle) or an unrealistic imagination. (Judging from my first year's growth, in 10 years I'll be able to....) Young investors are especially susceptible to such thoughts, particularly if the preceding generation—through hard work and strength—has inadvertently planted feelings of financial security and therefore a disincentive to perform.

Finally, don't get bogged down in emotional reactions, even to painful setbacks. Self-pity makes you think like a victim, and that is a position of weakness. Instead, use problems—even crises—as stimulants that prompt you to examine your behavior, gain objectivity, communicate with your financial advisor, and reevaluate your priorities. Just as our economy needs recessions to correct imbalances and dispose of overextensions, you need these "corrections" also! They present your best opportunity to test yourself, improve your strategies, and grow stronger with each experience.

Keep Your Eye on the Big Picture

Have a firm sense of what is important to you and act accordingly. At the top of the list is integrity because that drives all else. Integrity requires courage, and there's no getting around that. Have the fortitude to appraise yourself each day and take an inventory of your actions relative to your family, your career, your health, your character, and your relationship to society. Recognize that money is not an end, but a means to your ends: satisfying relationships, a loving family, and overall fulfillment.

The big picture requires you to think beyond yourself. Reducing waste, properly managing your health, and preserving the environment are examples of mutually economic advantages for you and society. The most important global view extends beyond us—to our children and eventually to their children. No matter how diligently we follow sensible rules, seek sound investment advice, take responsibility, plan ahead, and act with strength, this big picture will fade in time unless we find ways to instill in our children the knowledge, skills, and character they need to carry on with the wealth we have passed to them.

Make It Happen

Although I have been educated by my firm, my colleagues, the media, and of course, the markets, I must acknowledge that my greatest teachers have been my clients. When I entered the brokerage business, I was surprised when I had my first learning experiences with "real people!" At the time, I thought it was specific to my career, but later I realized that this is how all young professionals get started! Over the years, clients and I have grown together, learning from our mistakes and celebrating our achievements. There's nothing like a dramatic market downturn (and I've seen quite a few) to severely test an advisory relationship. The most significant lesson I've learned from my own clients is that it's about so much more than the money. I am forever grateful to them for teaching me what it *is* about—relationships and putting the clients' best interests first.

It's all up to you. Winners finish each day by asking, "What have I done today to live up to my potential?"

Be a winner. Make It Happen.

Formulas Used for Chapter 12 Calculations

You may find use for the formulas that underlie the calculations shown in this chapter. You can perform all these calculations on a simple calculator, but a more complex calculator can allow you to be more efficient. Several online financial calculators are available, such as www.dinkytown.net. Reminder: As noted in Chapter 12, "Expect to Pay a Price—Either Now or Later—for the Choices You Make About Handling Your Money," some rounding is done in these formulas.

Review of Step 3: Adjusting Your Monthly Financial Needs for 3% Inflation over 25 Years

Future Value (Estimated) of Today's $7,500 After 25 Years

Future Value = Present Value $(1 + \text{Inflation Rate})^{\text{Number of Years}}$

Future Value = $7,500 $(1.03)^{25}$

Future Value = $15,700

Review of Step 4: Calculating the Capital Investment Value Needed to Generate the $15,700 Monthly Draw ($188,000 Annually) Needed 25 Years from Now

Ending Balance Needed to Support a $15,700 Monthly Draw

$$\text{Ending Balance} = \frac{\text{Annual Income Withdrawal}}{\text{Withdrawal Rate}}$$

$$\text{Ending Balance} = \frac{\$188,000}{.05}$$

$$\text{Ending Balance} = \$3,760,000$$

Review of Step 6: Calculating the Future Value of $250,000 Today After 25 Years of Returns at a Rate of 7%

Future Value (Estimated) of Today's $250,000 in Liquid Assets

Total Future Value = Total Present Value $(1 + \text{Rate of Return})^{\text{Number of Years}}$

Total Future Value = $\$250,000 \, (1.07)^{25}$

Total Future Value = $\$1,356,858$

Review of Step 7: Calculating the Asset Gap Needing to Be Filled by Savings and Investment Returns over the Next 25 Years

Asset Gap at Retirement Before Additional Savings

Gap = Total Needed at Retirement Minus Today's
Investment Assets at Retirement

Gap = $3,760,000 – $1,356,858

Gap = $2,403,142

Review of Step 8: Calculating the Amount You Will Need to Save Annually for 25 Years to Close the Retirement Investment Gap

Annual Savings Needed to Bridge the Gap at Retirement

$$\text{Annual Savings Needed} = \frac{\text{Gap}}{\left[\dfrac{(1 + \text{Rate of Return})^{\text{Number of Years}} - 1}{\text{Rate of Return}}\right]}$$

$$\text{Annual Savings Needed} = \frac{\$2,403,142}{\left[\dfrac{(1.07)^{25} - 1}{.07}\right]}$$

$$\text{Annual Savings Needed} = \frac{\$2,403,142}{63.249038}$$

Annual Savings Needed = $37,995

Index

growth
  aggressive growth, investment
    objectives, 91-96
  income, investment
    objectives, 90
  investment objectives, 91
guidelines for finding an advisor
  who will give you care and
  quality, 137
gut reactions, recognizing and
  respecting, 126

H

hard assets, 61
health, 186
healthcare
  exercise, 189-192
  personal responsibility, 193
heart attacks, 195
hobbies, 43, 187

I-J-K

"ideal clients," 121
illiquidity, 46
incentives, 194-197
income
  adjusting for future inflation,
    105-107
  calculating ending balance you
    need to support inflated
    income figure, 108
  estimating desired income in
    today's dollars, 104
  with growth, investment
    objectives, 90
  investment objectives, 89

inflation, adjusting income for,
  105-107
influences, 198
insurance, survivorship, 196-197
integrity, 179, 183
  applying to life plans, 185-187
  evaluating yourself, 180-182
  moving from trying to doing,
    184-185
investigating character of people
  with whom you associate, 50-52
investing with friends, 69-70
investment objectives, 87
  aggressive growth, 91-96
  capital preservation, 88-89
  growth, 91
  income, 89
  income with growth, 90
  risk, 88
investment strategy, 60-64
investors
  defined, 2
  perceptions, 151-158
  succeeding as, 5-7

L

learning from mistakes, 26-27
lending money and not getting
  repaid, 81-86
life plans, integrity, 185-187
liquid, 46
liquid assets, estimating starting
  balance, 109
living the consequences of
  someone else's choices, 73

W

X-Y-Z

FINANCIAL TIMES

In an increasingly competitive world, it is quality of thinking that gives an edge—an idea that opens new doors, a technique that solves a problem, or an insight that simply helps make sense of it all.

We work with leading authors in the various arenas of business and finance to bring cutting-edge thinking and best-learning practices to a global market.

It is our goal to create world-class print publications and electronic products that give readers knowledge and understanding that can then be applied, whether studying or at work.

To find out more about our business products, you can visit us at www.ftpress.com.